# PRAISE FOR SUSAN'S WORK I

"Susan has a gift of giving women who have been batt[...] forward. This book is her best work yet, forging a clear path to a life of power and purpose for women who want to thrive in peace, love and joy!"

— Alyce LaViolette, MS, MFT, author, *It Could Happen to Anyone: Why Battered Women Stay*

"Susan's work has been developed from the heart and appeals to the emotions, the mind, and the subconscious. She has impacted the lives of countless women, helping them rethink and reimagine their experiences of being abused so they can recover their lives with dignity, success, and hope."

—Kathryn Tull, MA, LMFT, author, *Next Bold Step: Learning to Love and Value Yourself and Know That You Matter!*

"As a survivor of childhood abuse, Susan introduced me to a part of me that was untouched by all that happened to me. Now I'm more than a survivor, I am a thriver! Seeing the world through the eyes of a thriver is amazing! I am thankful for Susan's guidance that has gotten me here and how it helps me stay in the Thriver Zone every day."

—Teri Coughlin, My Avenging Angel Workshops™ participant

"Susan's work is impressive. I use her books in my practice, helping abuse survivors, young or old, move beyond survivor to thriver. Her materials can help all who have suffered trauma. I love how Susan's books incorporate a journey to healing without having my clients relive the trauma itself."

—Diana Barnes-Fox, MA, AMFT, ALPCC

## PRAISE FOR SUSAN FROM WOMEN IN HER WORKSHOPS

"Susan is an incredible woman! I thank her for providing me the opportunity to thrive."

—Lynne

"Susan has been there for me, connected me with other women, and encouraged me to seize opportunities to move forward with my life. Her work has helped me focus on my passions without fear and grounded me in a community of strong women who are my role models as I move forward as a thriver."

—Faye

"Susan's work has significantly broadened my perspective and opened me up to the Thriver in me, in all of us. It does require you to have a willingness to turn over old beliefs and thoughts for a new approach to dealing with one's self and others. I have learned to think of my goals with more enthusiasm and as something attainable vs. out of reach, which was my old conditioning."

—LOUISE

"Susan's work has helped me to overcome the fear and trauma associated with abuse. I have been able to step forward and know that I can survive and meet life's challenges head on. I know I have the heartfelt support of Susan and all the women in the thriver community. There, I am not alone nor am I judged."

—DIANNE

"Susan has helped me as a person to focus on the future. I have been able to define who I am, break out to freedom, and pursue creative passions. I have enjoyed the friendship of the women I have met in the Thriver community who have walked the same journey as mine."

—PAM

"Since working with Susan, I have been able to express myself through journaling, visioning, and dance. I've learned to love myself and others. I know how to free myself of worries, doubts, and fears. I have learned self-respect and how to respect others. I now have a purpose in my life! Living well is the best revenge."

—LAURIE

"I have used the tools and techniques that Susan has offered and developed new habits. I have a more positive perspective on who I am as a person. I have been reenergized, and I'm able to stay focused and be present in the moment, rather than the past. I have enjoyed warm, rich friendships with the women in the thriver community."

—ROBIN

"Through Susan's work, I have come to understand and overcome things that have weighed me down. What I have learned has strengthened me emotionally, and I have let others recovering from abuse to know that there are people like Susan who care and want us to succeed."

—NANCY

# Staying in the Thriver Zone

## A Road Map to Manifest a Life of Power and Purpose

Susan M. Omilian JD

*Reclaiming the Lives of Women*
*Who Have Been Abused*

Susan,
You are
thriving
8/2018

**Butterfly Bliss Productions LLC**
West Hartford, CT

**Staying in the Thriver Zone: A Road Map to Manifest a Life of Power and Purpose**

**Butterfly Bliss Productions LLC**
P.O. Box 330482, West Hartford, CT 06133
*ButterflyBlissProductions.com*
*ThriverZone.com*
*SusanOmilian.com*

ISBN # 978-0-9842509-4-3 printed book
ISBN # 978-0-9842509-5-0 e-book

Worksheets referenced in the text can be downloaded at "Resources" on *ThriverZone.com*.

Author photo by Cynthia Lang Photography
Maggie's photo by Joe Sherman | *PhotographicArtistry.net*
Front cover & interior design concept by Donna Gentile Creative | *DonnaGentileCreative.com*
Cover & interior production by Another Jones Graphics | *AnotherJones.com*

***A portion of the proceeds of this book will be donated to services for women and children who have experienced abuse and violence.***

This book is available at quantity discounts for bulk purchase. For information, contact the publisher.

Publisher's Cataloging-In-Publication Data
(Prepared by The Donohue Group, Inc.)

Names: Omilian, Susan M.
Title: Staying in the Thriver Zone : a road map to manifest a life of power and purpose / Susan M. Omilian JD.
Description: West Hartford, CT : Butterfly Bliss Productions LLC, [2018] | Series: [The Thriver Zone series] | "Reclaiming the lives of women who have been abused." | Includes bibliographical references and index.
Identifiers: ISBN 9780984250943 (print) | ISBN 9780984250950 (ebook)
Subjects: LCSH: Abused women--Psychology. | Self-actualization (Psychology) in women. | Control (Psychology) | Happiness. | Quality of life.
Classification: LCC HV6626 .O452 2018 (print) | LCC HV6626 (ebook) | DDC 362.8292--dc23

Printed in the United States of America

# DEDICATION

**Dedicated to my niece Maggie (1980 – 1999)
and all the women whose lives have been made better by her story.**

*I am no longer content to live a private life and concern myself only with affairs
that I perceive to affect me. The things I do in my public life can make a difference.
I foresee myself raising a family eventually, and I do not want to pass on to them
a world which I have made no attempt to better.*

—Reflections by Maggie in a college school paper

May your dream live on!
~ Susan M. Omilian ~

*Surviving is essential. Thriving is elegant.*

— MAYA ANGELOU

# ACKNOWLEDGMENTS

For all the women, survivors of abuse, who I have met and worked with for almost four decades, I admire your courage, persistence, and refusal to let what has happened to you define who you are. I have learned from you what it takes to stay in the Thriver Zone!

Thanks for blessing my life with your heartfelt stories.

A special thank you to the women who agreed to appear throughout this book and share their "thriver" stories of manifesting, creating a life of purpose, and reclaiming their power.

Thanks to Anita Jones, amazing book designer, Claudia Volkman for her keen eye in editing this book, and Sharon Castlen for her support, guidance, and remarkable vision in marketing this book.

Most of all, thanks to all who have let me share your journey as you have shared mine to discovering the life we were destined to live and the work that we were born to do.

There is no greater gift!

# ABOUT THE AUTHOR

An attorney, author, and motivational speaker, Susan Omilian has worked extensively as an advocate to end violence against women for the past forty years. In the 1970s, she founded a rape crisis center and represented battered women in divorce proceedings in the early 1980s. She also litigated sex discrimination cases including helping to articulate the legal concept that made sexual harassment illegal in the 1990s.

She is a published author of several books on sex discrimination law as well as articles for newspapers and journals, including *The Voice: The Journal of the Battered Women's Movement* published by the National Coalition Against Domestic Violence (NCADV). Susan holds a law degree from Wayne State University in Detroit and a bachelor of arts degree in journalism from the University of Michigan. She is licensed to practice law in both Connecticut and Michigan.

With the death of her nineteen-year-old niece Maggie, who was shot and killed in October 1999 by her ex-boyfriend, Susan's work on behalf of women became more personal and immediate. She vowed to help other women move on after abuse and create a new life for themselves and their children as Maggie could not.

Susan's other books in *The Thriver Zone Series*™ include *Entering the Thriver Zone: A Seven-Step Guide to Thriving After Abuse*, published in 2016. In 2017, Susan published a novel, *Awaken: The Awakening of the Human Spirit on a Healing Journey*, which is the first book in *The Best Revenge Series*™.

## SUSAN'S PERSONAL MISSION STATEMENT

*"I am a woman of power whose mission in life is to be a catalyst for change for victims of violence against women. Today I celebrate my life by building a community of strong, independent, productive women who have survived abuse and are thriving in well-being, love, and joy."*

# ABOUT THE SPEAKER

Susan Omilian is an experienced, inspirational speaker with a dramatic story and a unique motivational model to share. She has helped hundreds of women reclaim their lives after abuse and take the journey from victim to survivor to "thriver!"

As the award-winning originator and facilitator since 2001 of My Avenging Angel Workshops™ based on the idea that "living well is the best revenge," Susan has developed a seven-step process to thriving after abuse. It has been described as "life-changing" and as "a component for women recovering from abuse that has been virtually overlooked." Susan delivers her message of hope and possibility for women with passion and enthusiasm fueled by her own personal tragedy—her niece Maggie's violent death. It is her firm belief that women who take the journey to thriving are less likely to return to an abusive relationship or suffer the long-term physical and psychological consequences of the abuse they have experienced.

With simple, invigorating writing exercises and inspirational success stories, Susan's book, *Entering the Thriver Zone: A Seven-Step Guide to Thriving After Abuse* sets forth the motivational guidance she has successfully used with women over the last fifteen years. Susan envisions that millions of women who have faced violence and abuse as well as their families, friends, counselors, therapists, and healthcare providers will find her first book in *The Thriver Zone Series*™ an invaluable guide to taking the life-changing journey from victim to survivor to thriver!

Susan is a recognized, articulate national expert on the process of recovery after violence and abuse. She has been invited to speak throughout the country by victim rights organizations such as National Organization of Victim Assistance (NOVA), before service providers and clinicians as well as to students and faculty on college campuses. She has also been a keynote speaker at domestic violence and sexual assault awareness events and a featured presenter at national meetings and international conferences sponsored by the Institute on Violence, Abuse and Trauma (IVAT).

Susan also regularly speaks to diverse audiences, including a Pennsylvania women's prison, where her books and materials have been used with women inmates to help them to break the cycle of abuse in their lives. Her books have been purchased throughout the United States and in countries including Netherlands, New Zealand, Canada, South Africa, and American Samoa. Susan works with Indian tribes in California who, like others interested in her materials, have purchased multiple copies of her books and used them with individuals and groups in clinical and therapeutic settings as well as in victim assistance programs.

Susan's company, Butterfly Bliss Productions LLC, which publishes her non-fiction books and novels, is also developing an imprint, *Thriver Spirit Press*, to publish books and stories that epitomize the healing and inspirational energy of moving beyond struggle and abuse.

For more information about Susan's transformational work or to arrange for her to speak, please visit *ThriverZone.com*.

# CONTENTS

My heart is moved by all that I cannot save:
so much has been destroyed.
I have to cast my lot with those who,
age after age,
perversely with no extraordinary power,
reconstitute the world.

– ADRIENNE RICH

# NOTE FROM THE AUTHOR –
# THE JOURNEY CONTINUES

On October 18, 1999, Maggie, my brother's nineteen-year-old stepdaughter, was murdered on a college campus by her ex-boyfriend, who then killed himself.

Shock, guilt, and a cry for revenge welled up inside me, but what was I to do? I couldn't save Maggie. No one had seen the danger she was in after she ended the relationship, not even Maggie herself. He had never physically assaulted or threatened her, and she didn't know he had a gun. Although I had worked as an attorney and advocate for women for many years, I too had missed the warning signs in the relationship., my long-standing work to end violence against women became more personal and immediate. I was determined to turn Maggie's tragic death into an opportunity to help other women move on with their lives after abuse as Maggie could not.

In the nearly two decades since Maggie's death, I have worked with hundreds of women who have experienced domestic violence, sexual assault, and child abuse and helped them take the journey from victim to survivor to thriver. These women long to move beyond the abuse, violence, and trauma in their lives, but they don't know how to make that happen.

This is the work I was born to do, and now I do it in Maggie's memory.

How do I do it? First, I developed a seven-step guide that helps women see their journey and find the positive, thriver energy inside them again. Second, I have crafted a motivational model that moves their positive energy into focused desires so they can manifest their dreams and find their real, authentic selves. With these tools, women have done remarkable things! They have gone back to school, gotten new, better jobs, started singing again, bought their first homes, and most of all, many have found new healthy, loving relationships.

They have entered the Thriver Zone and learned how to stay there so they can regain their power and find purpose in the fabulous life that lies ahead of them. I am so proud of them!

I hope that this book, the second in *The Thriver Zone Series*™ following *Entering the Thriver Zone: A Seven-Step Guide to Thriving After Abuse*, will provide you with all you need to find a life of peace, joy, and freedom as a thriver!

—Susan M. Omilian JD

# HOW TO USE THIS BOOK

## YES, YOU ARE A WRITER!

You can do the writing exercises in this book that will take you through **The Road Map for the Journey to the Real YOU!™.** If you are afraid someone might see what you have written, write on a piece of paper and then destroy it. You don't have to keep what you write. Just get it out there for a while and let it shine!

## WORKING FROM WRITING PROMPTS IS EASY!

When you see ✍ throughout this book, it means it's time to write from a "writing prompt!" A writing prompt is simply a way into your writing. Let it take you where it will, even if what you write has nothing to do with the prompt. Keep writing. Don't stop!

Don't worry about spelling, grammar, or if what you wrote makes any sense! If you like printable copies of the worksheets in this book, go to *ThriverZone. com* and click on WORKSHEETS.

## DECORATE YOUR OWN JOURNAL.

Before you start writing, buy yourself a journal or notebook and decorate the cover! Use pictures from magazines or photos from your own life as well as stickers or glitter glue to bling it up! You deserve it! It's your Thriver Zone Journal to write in and keep.

## INVITE A FRIEND TO JOIN YOU! FORM YOUR OWN THRIVER GROUP!

Get together with a group of your friends and THRIVE! Visit *ThriverZone.com* to learn how. Find more writing prompts and exercises there. You can work through this book by yourself or invite a friend or group of friends to do it with you. Writing, reading, and sharing the experience with other women is a fabulous thing to do.

## THERE ARE NO RULES!

You can't do this wrong! Don't worry—you can do it! Visit *ThriverZone.com* to learn how.You will also find more writing prompts and exercises there. ENJOY!

# Getting Started

## A ROAD MAP TO MANIFEST A LIFE OF POWER AND PURPOSE

*With deliberate intention, fueled by POSITIVE ENERGY*
*and EMOTION, you can have what you DESIRE.*
*PUSH through your FEARS and RESISTANCE*
*and find the REAL YOU in a Life of POWER and PURPOSE!*

Are you a dreamer?

Do you often have wild, crazy dreams about how you want your life to be going forward? Do you long for a future with limitless possibilities for you and your family? Don't we all want that fairy-tale "happy ending" we were promised?

I know. I'm a dreamer, too. I have been one ever since I was a kid. And I'm a lover of fairy tales. I'd love to have a "happy ending" in my life!

Funny, have you ever noticed that sometimes one of your dreams will come true in the most unexpected way? And you are amazed. Wow! I'm so lucky, you think. Then at other times something you have wanted and waited for a long time doesn't get realized no matter how hard you try. So sometimes this dreaming the big dream works and sometimes it doesn't.

But how does it work? Is it really magic or is there a method to it? Could some process to make your dreams come true work for you? I have an answer on that. Not that I'm so smart, but I have observed in my own life and in how the Universe works around me that there is a natural process we human beings go through to manifest our deepest desires and wildest dreams. The components to that process sometimes all work together and voila! Other times we get stuck in one place or the other, and none of it works.

Why doesn't it work sometimes? For those of us who have experienced abuse and violence in our lives, the trauma caused by those acts can cause us to lose all hope of any success in our lives and derail our dreams, no matter what the process. But I do believe – and I want to share with you in this book why I believe – that whatever we dream can be ours, no matter what our circumstances, past experiences, or current stage in life. Young or old, rich or poor, smart or not so smart, we can manifest what we desire, particularly if our values and strongest passions match our wildest dreams.

Let me give you an example from my own life as to how this can work.

## IMPACT OF MAGGIE'S DEATH

In October 1999, my nineteen-year-old niece Maggie was killed on a college campus by her abusive and possessive ex-boyfriend who then killed himself. While I had worked on violence against women as an attorney and advocate for two decades prior, with Maggie's death I felt a more immediate and personal need to make a difference. If I couldn't change what happened to Maggie, I wanted to help other women who did survive abusive relationships to move on and have the best life ever. So, with positive energy and a strong passion for the work, I focused my desire on starting a program in 2001 that I called the My Avenging Angel Workshops™. The workshop name was based on the idea that "living well is the best revenge," and that's what I wanted for myself. The man who killed my niece destroyed her and her chance for a wondrously full and happy adult life, but he was not going to destroy me. I wanted to find a way to shift the paradigm and find opportunity for myself and others in this tremendous loss.

But what was I thinking? I had no experience conducting workshops for abused women, no funding, and certainly little idea if I would even be successful. To tell the truth, the first session of my first workshop wasn't so great, but I didn't give up. Somehow – maybe it is magical! – people showed up to help me and things evolved. My second workshop was more successful, and by the end of it, I saw the women who attended it transform their lives in significant ways. They filed for divorce and left abusive relationships, went back to school to follow their career dreams, and took on challenges like whitewater rafting just to get positive energy flowing in their lives again.

It was amazing! I never dreamed that I could make something like that happen. But I did! How? First, I focused on my desire to do a workshop to help women take the journey from victim to survivor to thriver. Then I fueled that desire with positive energy and a deep passion for the work I truly wanted to do. So I invited women who had survived abuse to come and take this journey to thriving with me. But it was also an invitation to myself to move beyond the pain and loss of Maggie's death and do more than just survive. I could thrive too!

## VICTIM ⇨ SURVIVOR ⇨ THRIVER

With all this positive energy and the passion I have for this work, I pushed through any fears or limiting beliefs I had about myself and my skills to conduct these workshops. And when the workshops succeeded, I felt an overwhelming rush of pure joy and pleasure that I could do such meaningful work, that helped and healed others. In time the workshops became more and more successful and I could feel my "Real YOU" (a concept we'll explore more later in this book) being fed by my work. Discovering my authentic self in this process was a big surprise. I didn't realize that there was a strong, vibrant part of me that was untouched by all that had ever happened to me or my niece Maggie. Feeding that spiritual part of me was so rewarding that I kept doing my workshops, helping more and more women as my work expanded and flourished.

Soon I had a new focused desire to write a book about the amazing work I was doing. Yes, I had a lot of fear and anxiety about succeeding at that too. But once again I fueled the process with positive energy and a strong belief that I could, so I broke down that wall of resistance. When my first book – *Entering the Thriver Zone: A Seven Step Guide to Thriving After Abuse* – was published, I again felt the rush and exhilaration of the Real YOU inside me. That voice told me, *You did good. This is important. It can change the lives of so many women.* And I believed it. YES!

## A ROAD MAP FOR YOU

Here I am now with this book, ready to expand the reach of my work once more and articulate a process for you, my readers, that I now call ***The Road Map for the Journey to the Real YOU!*™**. As I have been on this amazing journey, I want to offer you the chance to experience it too. You may have already had an experience like mine. Maybe a focused desire of yours was realized by giving it a lot of positive energy and pushing through your fear to get it done. But you may not have realized the full power and potential of this process. Yes, it is amazing to manifest a desire that can transform your life, but it can also be overwhelming and scary. It takes a great deal of courage and strength to push through your fears and resistance. Some would rather give up than face fear, or worse, defeat in not being able to overcome the fear.

My gift to you in this book is to make you more aware of this process and use it more consciously and successfully in your life. I don't want to make it feel less magical for you, because there is magic in it! But I do want you to have access to this way of manifesting your desires and finding the Real YOU in your life that is truly transformational.

Why is it important to find the Real YOU?

- **We can find out who we are!** Manifesting our dreams and finding the Real YOU helps us identify what interests and passions excite and nourish us.

- **That knowledge is power!** It can heal our broken parts and reveal more of the part of us that is untouched by all that has ever happened to us.

- **That power can help us find the true purpose of our lives.** Why are we here? What can we accomplish? What will we leave behind? By exploring what feeds our Real YOU, we can consciously direct ourselves into a life of power and purpose despite all that has happened to us.

- **In finding a life of purpose, we move closer to living well as our best revenge!** Living a life that is fulfilling to us and of great value and service to others could be our "happy ending!"

## FINDING YOUR WORK

Since the murder of my nineteen-year-old niece, I have indeed found the work I was destined to do in this lifetime – helping women who have been abused take the journey from victim to survivor to thriver! That journey has transformed my life as it has transformed the lives of many of the women I have worked with. We enter the Thriver Zone to find that we really are on that journey to reclaiming our lives. If we stay in the Thriver Zone, we can manifest our desires and find the Real YOU in a life of power and purpose. Then our work in this lifetime becomes our life and our life is our work.

Here's an example of how this process works:

Some women I have worked with started their journey to thriving by manifesting a desire such as going back to school and adding to their skills and abilities. With this additional schooling, the women have gotten new or better jobs – another manifestation. For some, these jobs involved teaching children or being a social worker – positions in which they could greatly influence girls and young women. In encouraging these young people to pursue more opportunities in their own lives and not get involved in an abusive relationship, the women manifested even more and began to create a life for themselves of true purpose in helping others. A few who felt comfortable identifying themselves as former victims of violence, shared with the young people their personal journey beyond abuse. In doing so, they became role models for these girls, young women, as well as boys and young men that we all can survive and thrive!

You can see in the above example how each new manifestation along the way keeps us in the Thriver Zone, as we work to avail ourselves of opportunities to define (or redefine) the purpose of our lives despite the violence, abuse, and trauma we have experienced. We can't change what has happened to us, but we can transform how we see these experiences and how they shape our lives. We take this journey to a life of power and purpose.

## MANIFESTING YOUR DESIRES

If manifesting your desires is at the core of this journey to thriving and can lead you to finding a life of power and purpose, let's explore more what it means to "manifest." A dictionary definition of the word *manifest* is "to clearly reveal something to the mind, sight, understanding or other senses." Let's look at other, diverse views of it.

- *You are here to manifest your innate enlightenment.*

    – Morihei Ueshiba, a martial artist, founder of Japanese art of aikido

- *We were born to manifest the glory of God that is within us.*

    – Marianne Williamson, a spiritual leader in A Course in Miracles

- *Life is about, every single day, getting up to manifest your truth.*

    – Cory Booker, U.S. Senator from New Jersey

For some women it will be a major accomplishment after leaving an abusive relationship or dealing with sexual assault to manifest any desire, even something as simple as getting out of bed, seeing friends, or keeping their job. But it could also be a wish to go back to school or find a new or better job that could take their lives to a new and better place. Then the test is pushing through their fears and accomplishing something they thought they could never do. The feeling of exhilaration for the Real YOU when someone accomplishes that kind of goal is really the reward for taking the journey beyond abuse. Is it worth it? Yes! That's because thriving is an amazing state of mind and being!

Once you enter the Thriver Zone, you'll need a road map to stay in the Thriver Zone so you can manifest your wildest desires and find the Real YOU inside! And the ultimate goal of manifesting is to discover a life of power and purpose – the life of a thriver!

What is a thriver? Here's my working definition:

*A thriver is a happy, self-confident and productive individual who believes she has a prosperous life ahead of her. She is primed to follow her dreams, go back to school, find a new job, start her own business, or write her story. She believes in herself and in her future so much that she will not return to an abusive relationship. She speaks knowledgeably and confidently about her experiences and is not stuck in her anger or need for revenge.*

*Living well is her best revenge!*

With *The Road Map for the Journey to the Real YOU!™* set forth in this book, I invite you to take the journey to thriving and finding a life of power and purpose. But each of you will do this journey differently, and you may have many more obstacles to overcome than others. Just as I have heard that it takes a woman seven times to leave an abusive relationship, it may take some time and some healing before you can fully move beyond the abuse in your life.

What I have learned from my own experience and in working with women over the years is that the biggest barriers that keep us down are those that keep us from feeling positive about ourselves and our future lives. These obstacles put our fears right in front of us and dare us to get by, past, or through them to the other side.

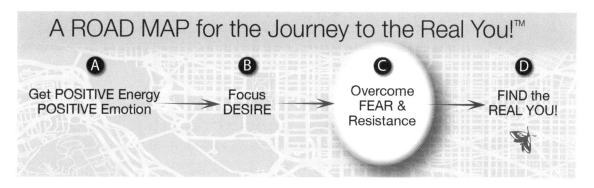

A ROAD MAP for the Journey to the Real You!™

A — Get POSITIVE Energy POSITIVE Emotion → B — Focus DESIRE → C — Overcome FEAR & Resistance → D — FIND the REAL YOU!

That's another reason why I love the quote: *"Living well is the best revenge."* After all, isn't getting on with one's life the most exacting revenge against those who have beaten us down and told us we are nothing? But it is hard to face our stories! We will be judged about them. Can't you just hear the comments? *Why didn't you leave sooner? How could you be with such a man? What were you thinking?* We will also try to avoid the social stigma and shame of having been once abused or assaulted. Because of these kind of fears, I have purposefully not asked you in the exercises and activities in this book to disclose or relive anything about the abuse you have experienced in the past. But you can feel comfortable knowing that you are not alone in the circle; others have had similar struggles.

As a woman who has experienced abuse in the past, you may also face costly ongoing legal battles with your abusive ex-partner on such issues as property division, child custody, and child support. You may have substance abuse issues in your life as a result of the abuse, have little or no education, or no job or a low-paying job with little financial backing or support from your family or friends. Your culture or religion may also judge you about leaving a partner or marriage even if your partner is abusive to you. Finally, you may fear the possibility that you will return to an abusive relationship. Will you see the warning signs of abuse the next time around? Will a healthy, happy relationship ever come your way? These are real fearful thoughts!

But don't worry! You can overcome all these obstacles and learn more in this book about how to stay on course and thrive after abuse. First, as I described in my book *Entering the Thriver Zone: A Seven Step Guide to Thriving After Abuse,* you can be open to the possibility that there is a life beyond abuse – more than just surviving, but thriving. The steps I lay out in that book can get you on the path to thriving. But what I'll show you in this book is how to go deeper into that journey to thriving so that you can stay in the Thriver Zone and regain your power and find purpose in this life.

## THE MOTIVATIONAL MODEL TO USE

***The Road Map for the Journey to the Real YOU!*™** is the motivational model that I have used successfully to keep my own life moving forward and find the work I was born to do. With this model, I have been able not merely to survive all the difficult things that have happened to me, including the violent and tragic death of Maggie, my niece, but I also have moved on to find a life of purpose helping others!

While I realize now that I have known this model all my life, it was only in trying to cope with Maggie's death that I became more aware of the natural process underlying it. Now I use it more consciously, and in doing so, I have uncovered my hidden talents, found the focus of my creative potential, and transformed my life in a positive, productive way. In the process, I have found the unique and innovative work that I do with women who have been abused, and, despite what happened to Maggie, I have been able to:

- *discover opportunity in what I had considered as loss*
- *find positive energy to push myself forward*
- *dare to create the life I want, and,*
- *overcome my fears to find the dynamic Real YOU inside me.*

After a quick introduction to the model in this chapter, the rest of this book will show you step-by-step – or Map Point-by-Map Point – how you can also use this Road Map to change and transform your life. I would love to see you transform and take such an amazing and exciting process. Wouldn't that be wonderful? Come with me, and we'll explore ***The Road Map for the Journey to the Real YOU!*™**.

Does that sound exciting? It is! In fact, it is magical! I have helped hundreds of women use this Road Map on their journey, and they all have found it so amazing that when they get there, they always ask me, "Why didn't anyone tell us about this before? Why are we only finding out about this now?" I don't know the answer to those "why" questions, but I do know that there is a way to get there, so let's just let the magic happen. Don't feel shortchanged if you don't feel like you have ever been there in your life. Now is your chance, and you are in for a real thrill.

What is great about this ***The Road Map for the Journey to the Real YOU!*™** is that whenever I feel like I've lost my way, I can get out my map and see where I am stuck. Maybe I have to slow down a little or avoid a detour and then get back on the road to success. Over time, I have gone from only contacting my Real YOU for a few minutes each day to spending whole days, weeks, and even months in her wondrous company. In fact, what I have found is that connecting with our authentic selves is not that hard. It's just that when something really good happens to us, we think we are just lucky or that the stars in the heavens have lined up for once. If we see someone else getting what she desires, we think she is just special or has some "in" with the powers that be. But the process of making our dreams come true is how the Universe works, and the sooner we learn how to use it more consciously, the sooner we will be living in the Real YOU – our Happy Ending! – every single moment of our lives.

Enough talking about it. Let's do it!

Here is your point-by-point guide to staying in the Thriver Zone – ***The Road Map for the Journey to the Real YOU!*™**

Enjoy the ride! Let's manifest some of your dreams here . . . YES!

~ ~ ~ ~ ~ ~ ~ ~ ~ ~ ~ ~ ~ ~

***When we bring what is within out***
***into the world, miracles happen.***
– HENRY DAVID THOREAU

*Always remember,*

*you have within you*

*the strength, the patience,*

*and the passion*

*to reach for the stars to*

*change the world.*

— HARRIET TUBMAN

# Map Point A

## GET POSITIVE ENERGY

*Your positive action combined with*
*positive thinking results in success.*

— SHIV KHERA

## POSITIVE ENERGY AND EMOTION:

- **You have a degree of energy and emotion to exert at various times in your life.**

- **Sometimes your energy is high; other times it is low. At times you may feel you have a lot of problems and little hope that the future will be any better.**

- **Reenergizing yourself is an important part of the process. To do so, you may need to quiet negative thoughts and connect with the Happy Person Inside.**

- **Focusing on positive emotions like joy, happiness, and peace can propel you forward into your bright, brilliant future that you so richly deserve.**

*Beware of allowing a tactless word, a rebuttal,*
*a rejection to obliterate the whole sky.*

— ANAIS NIN

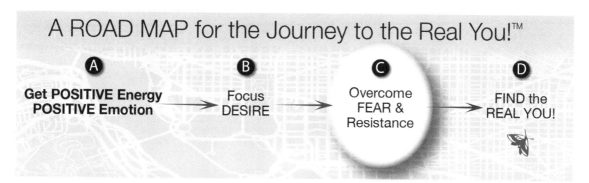

## MAP POINT A — Fueling Our Lives with Positive Energy

***The Road Map for The Journey to the Real YOU!™*** invites you to begin by bringing pure, positive energy into your life. As women who have been abused, we may be more familiar with the "victim" part of our lives. There we are fueled by negative thoughts and emotions such as anger, depression, resentment, and sadness. We may feel better when we move from "victim" to "survivor," but often we go through life always feeling like the victim or we spend all our energy merely surviving each new difficulty in our lives. Our mantra becomes "I can survive anything," and so we do, but we never really thrive. Remember the first part of our working definition of a thriver.

*A thriver is a happy, self-confident, and productive individual*
*who believes she has a prosperous life ahead of her.*

Notice all those positive words to describe the thriver energy – we feel happy, confident, productive, and prosperous. Even women who have been abused and violently assaulted can experience and stay in this kind of positive energy. For this **Map Point A,** we will concentrate on how to bring positive energy and emotion into our lives. Remember, it is our choice to stay in our positive thoughts or wallow in negative ones.

First, let's quiet the negative voice in our head that may be yelling a lot at this moment about how being positive is just not possible – too much bad stuff has happened to us; there is no hope for life getting any better!

## THE EXERCISE: QUIET THE INNER CRITIC

*If you gave your inner genius*
*as much credence as your inner critic,*
*you would be light years ahead of*
*where you stand now.*

—ALAN COHEN

This is a very powerful exercise (also included as one of the Seven Steps to Thriving After Abuse) that you can use to quiet negative voice in your head that constantly criticizes you and all that you do. Often this voice can drown out positive thoughts, so it is very important to calm this beast at the start.

The Inner Critic is usually a voice from our childhood, maybe coming from a parent or someone in authority over us who would say things to us like:

*"Stand up straight."*

*"Don't eat all that candy. You'll get sick."*

*"Go to sleep now. You have school in the morning."*

These messages were probably meant to protect us when we were young and teach us to take good care of ourselves as we grew older. But as adults, the voice will dictate all the "shoulds" and "should nots" in our lives without giving us a chance to speak against or contradict the things it comes up with. This voice can become very critical, overprotective, and at times, abusive and mean. Often, if a woman is in an abusive relationship, her partner will take on the voice of the inner critic and say cruel and nasty things to her like:

*"You are stupid, fat, and ugly."*

*"You'll never find anyone to love you as I do."*

*"You are a bad mother, and the house is a mess."*

It's easy for us to believe this voice and all or most of what it says. What the Inner Critic does is fuel our fears and insecurities and block us from taking positive, creative risks in our lives. It is very clever and knows exactly how to get to us. Such negative self-talk will always be with us. But we can learn to turn it down and lower the volume of the negative and bring up the alternate positive, affirming voice in your head.

Here is an exercise designed to quiet even the fiercest Inner Critic!

Take a moment to close your eyes and let yourself hear the critical voice inside your head. It may be a voice from your childhood – your mother or father or a teacher – and it may be male or female. Let it speak about your life for a moment without blocking out what it says.

Now open your eyes, and draw a line down the page of your journal or notebook.

✍ **PROMPT:** Make a list in the left-hand column of your Inner Critic's chatter.

Perhaps it is a word, a phrase, or a simple sentence. Whatever it is saying, let it out and put it on the page! Read the list aloud, then close your eyes again and listen for anything else to add. When you are done, take a deep breath, close your eyes, and let that voice go.

🖎 **PROMPT:** In the right-hand column, write a response to your Inner Critic.

Be strong, affirming, and positive in your responses. You can be feisty too, responding with "Who cares?" or "Not true!" If your Inner Critic says you're a bad mother, your response is "I'm a great mother!" Respond to each remark until your list looks like the one below. Even if your Inner Critic is saying so, you can't do this wrong!

| INNER CRITIC | YOUR RESPONSE |
| --- | --- |
| I'm fat, stupid, and ugly. | I am beautiful just the way I am. |
| I deserve to be treated badly. | No one deserves to be abused. |
| Nobody has ever really loved me. | I am loved and lovable! |
| I'm not good enough. | I am enough! |
| I'm wasting my time. | My time is my own. |
| I should be cleaning my house! | Housework can wait! |
| I'm a failure. I never do anything right. | I am perfect as I am. |

Use this Inner Critic Exercise regularly to keep yourself in the Thriver Zone, particularly when you take on a new project. You'll want to know what your Inner Critic has to say about it before you start – or when you feel stuck in one place or another. You need to know that you have a response to whatever it sends your way.

Many women I have worked with on this journey to thriving have found that quieting the Inner Critic has been essential for them not only to Enter the Thriver Zone, but also to Stay in the Thriver Zone. Look at some of their comments below:

### Quieting the Inner Critic can help you to . . .

*. . . feel grounded. Because of the abuse, I have lots of anxiety, and positive energy can easily be drained away from me. But with each day that passes, my vision of a great new life gets clearer. Now I surround myself with good, positive energy and look for the good inside me. Although my journey through this has been slow, I am now in positive energy, and I have my dignity and self-respect back.* – Susan

*... combat the negatives of that inner voice with positive truth. I am also surrounding myself with positive, nonjudgmental people who lift me up and support me.* – Jodie

*... keep my focus on a positive definition of myself. To do this, I have an Inner Critic chart [like one on previous page] handy in a notebook and whenever I hear negative criticism or words from others or negative thoughts from myself, I write them down and then my positive response. I do this with pens in multiple colors and I reread the positive so I can keep myself feeling happy, strong, and positive, not like a victim of anyone anymore.* – Cathryn

## THE EXERCISE: CREATE AFFIRMATIONS

Another way to quiet the Inner Critic and keep the positive energy flowing is to create affirmations about you and your life.

Read down the right-hand column of your list of positive responses to the Inner Critic's remarks in your notebook. Are there any affirming statements that particularly speak to you? Looking back at my sample, there are several great affirmations:

*I am loved and lovable.*
*I am becoming the person I truly want to be.*
*I am beautiful just the way I am.*
*I am perfect as I am.*

Here's more from the women:

*I am a beautiful person.*
*I have something. I'm going somewhere!*
*I am taking care of myself.*
*I am making good choices.*
*I am my true self.*
*I am whole and complete.*
*I am strong and courageous.*
*I am powerful.*
*I am worthy of love and friendship.*

These are called "affirmations" because they are declaring something that is true about us in the most positive way at the present time. You wouldn't say in an affirmation "I'm trying to take care of myself," but rather "I am healthy and happy." It's not that "I will be somebody someday," it is "I am somebody today."

Affirmations can also be statements you can grow into, something to challenge and stretch you into what you truly want to become. One affirmation that you may not be able to feel today but could move into is "I am a thriver." Let yourself feel your energy going in that direction each time you say those words.

✍ **PROMPT:** Write your affirmations on sticky notes using a thick black marker or crayon and display around your house. The bathroom mirror is a great spot so that you see them every morning. Or put them on or next to your computer monitor so you look at them often.

Believe in your affirmations! Go BIG with them and get strong!

## THE EXERCISE: WHAT MAKES YOU HAPPY

There is a Happy Person Inside You who is just waiting to get out. She is a thriver, and she is fabulous!

Not only can she counter the voice of the Inner Critic, but she is also your best cheerleader. She loves you, loves you, loves you unconditionally! She is the best side of you – a thriver – and she is YOU!

Each time we connect with this part of us, we are truly living our Happy Ending, the one we explored in the first book, *Entering the Thriver Zone: A Seven Steps to Thriving After Abuse.*

In that book, we explored how fairy tales and stories from our childhood can lead us to see how we can live our Happy Ending today. The best part of our lives can be right now if we can get the Happy Person Inside – our Thriver Energy – to come out and stay out in full force!

Can you imagine how that would feel? To me, it would be like coming home to a place within me that is easy and peaceful. It is a place where all is well, and all is possible. There I have no doubts or fears and no sense of longing. From there all will unfold as it should. When I lose contact with that strong, positive part of me, I can easily get lost, scared, confused, and feel very alone. My world comes apart, and I am separated from what is good, kind, and loving, not only to others but also to myself.

Another way I think about this special "Happy Place" is that there I can feel the part of me that has been untouched by all that has ever happened to me. I found the quote below with more about this place:

*In every one of us there is a safe island we can go to. Every time you go to that island with mindful breathing, you create a space of relaxation, concentration and insight. If you dwell on that island in yourself with mindful breathing, you are safe. That is a place where you can take refuge whenever you feel fearful, uncertain or confused.*

— BUDDHA

I like to go to that Happy Place where I feel safe and full of joy. To get myself there, I often consciously do something that makes me happy and then write about it. It's a powerful exercise. Here's how it works.

✎**PROMPT:** Write about something that makes you happy. Describes how it feels before, during, and after you do it.

It doesn't have to be anything really big, extravagant, or expensive. It could be going to the movies, baking cupcakes, or playing with your children. Whatever! Maybe you do this on a regular basis or you haven't done it in a long time. If you can do it now, that would be great. If not, then remember what it felt like the last time you did it.

Here's an example below for you that I did about what makes me happy:

**WHAT MAKES ME HAPPY – Sitting by the ocean makes me happy . . .**

**BEFORE I FEEL OR TELL MYSELF:** *I really don't have time to do this. It's too far for me to travel. I really don't need to do it. I don't have the money for gas.*

**DURING I FEEL OR TELL MYSELF:** *Gosh, this does feel really nice. I can feel myself relaxing. It takes me away from my problems and troubles. Water has a calming effect on me. I like being here. I have made a good choice. Why didn't I come here sooner?*

**AFTER I FEEL OR TELL MYSELF:** *That was great! I'm going to do that again soon. I feel so energized, so happy, so positive about everything in my life. I can take it all on now. What a great gift this is for me! I love how I am feeling, so creative. New thoughts are coming now. I* *have a plan for dealing with things I couldn't handle before. This is the best thing I've done for myself in a long time.*

Here's another What Makes Me Happy piece. It was written by Tennille, a woman who I worked with recently. She was inspired to do something that made her happy but hadn't done in a while. This is a fun piece!

*I had been telling myself that I wanted to or needed to start working out again. I had been giving myself so many excuses: "You can't afford a gym membership right now," or "You'll get dizzy and pass out and embarrass yourself."*

*I had a lot of self-doubt, but one Sunday I said, "Self, you are going to do it." I got ready to go for a run, putting on my stretch pants, sneakers, and a hoodie. I stretched out, kind of, before I went outside, and that's when I realized I was more out of shape than I thought. I hadn't even started to run, and I was already breaking out a sweat. Oh my God, I thought, this is going to hurt.*

*My daughter woke up, came into the room, and asked, "What are you doing?"*

*I said, "Going for a run."*

*"A what?" was her response.*

*Nevertheless, I popped my ear buds in, cranked up Mary J. Blige music, and ran down the stairs. My heart was pounding. I opened the door, and the cold, wet fog outside smacked me in the face. I stepped briskly. I thought, As soon as I reach the bottom of the hill, I am going to go for it! Some neighbors glanced at me awkwardly, as if to say, "We never saw her dressed like that."*

*LOL! I didn't care!*

*As soon as the town cemetery came into view, I lifted one foot and then the other. I let my arms swing, and I picked up the pace. I took a deep breath and, man! did it burn! I coughed, and my eyes filled with tears. Shake it off, I told myself, and I took even breaths instead. At this point I was halfway through the cemetery, and I wanted to turn back so bad! But just to impress myself, I kept going, and I read the names on the tombstones as I ran. How ironic that I chose this route. My mind began to drift. I thought of loved ones I had lost. I said prayers for them, hoping they were resting in paradise.*

*Then, without even realizing it, I was running. The mixed emotions gave me a surge of energy. My breathing had become steady. I almost glanced back, but at that very moment, a big red stop sign appeared, as if to say, STOP! NO LOOKING OR GOING BACK. Keep moving forward!*

*I kept moving. I kept moving past the cemetery, past the drugstore, past the church, and past the library, the post office, the town hall, the police department, the senior citizen center, the barber shop, and the pet store. I was whizzing by everything! Yes, I thought, you got this! The burning in my legs was bittersweet. My throat was dry, but my mind was so clear. I felt strong; I felt proud; I felt like a runner!*

*As I approached my complex, I slowed down. I jogged, then skipped, and finally walked. I reached my front door and looked at the device on my wrist. I had completed two miles. My heart rate was 140 bpm, and the smile on my face was priceless.*

*"We will be doing this again," I told myself, amazed at the confidence I had gained from my run. So later that Sunday, I rocked a black dress with black stockings and heels (appropriate, I promise) as I reintroduced my killer calves and legs to the world!*

*– TENNILLE*

## WHAT IF? – COMBINING APPROACHES

What if you try both approaches at the same time? What if you could Quiet Your Inner Critic and do What Makes Me Happy at the same time?

Wonderful, I'd say! Let's see how that would work.

This is a story from Adrienne, one of the women I have worked with over the years, helping her Enter the Thriver Zone and then Stay in the Thriver Zone so she could move forward on her thriver goals.

**Here's what she wrote:**

*Recently I had the opportunity to do something I LOVE. I got hired to facilitate a Laughter Yoga session, and I got paid for it! The job came to me effortlessly; my friend got the call and passed it on to me. The location was a Senior Center in a town I wasn't that familiar with about forty minutes from my home.*

**How I Felt Before – The Inner Critic:**

*OMG! Why did you take this job? You'll be driving there in rush hour traffic and in the dark! You are not even sure where it is. You could – and probably WILL – get lost.*

*You'll be late. It's twenty miles away! On the other side of the river! Your car will break down. Why do you have such an old car? If you don't study what you plan to do, you will flop. If you study too much, you will freeze up and flop.*

*No one will want to laugh with you. They won't like Laughter Yoga. What if you forget the exercises? You know how you forget things when you are flooded with oxygen.*

**How I Felt During – The Days Before:**

*I remind myself that I have a positive thriver response to all stress that my Inner Critic is creating here. I know I can break through my fear and agoraphobia.*

*The day before, I take a ride in the afternoon while it is still light to see where the venue is and how to get there. I promise myself I will not overstudy. I confirm the event, and I concentrate all week on feeling joy that I am going to laugh with a group and bring up my positive energy whenever I can.*

*I chant, "Ho Ho, Ha Ha Ha, Very Good, Very Good, Yea," and clap my hands often to bring up the energy. I feel as much gratitude as I can for everything in my life. I say my prayers.*

**How I Felt During – The Day of:**

*I review my Laughter Yoga manuals, gather the materials I have been using for years, and make some new handouts. I decide what to wear. This is important because, as a Laughter Yoga leader, I am really performing. I put all my things by the door with my map to the location on top. I work in the yard in the morning, connecting to nature and moving about physically. I take a shower, eat, check the traffic, and leave early – the event doesn't begin until 6:30 p.m., but I arrive at 6:15 p.m. The trip is slow, but I am feeling fine, and I am calm. When I arrive, nine women are there, all seniors, and we laugh and connect. Laughter Yoga always make me feel wonderful. We finish right at 7:30 p.m., and I am done!*

**How I Felt – After:**

> *I feel I did a good job, but maybe it could have been better. I will try not to judge and only focus on constructive criticism. The session flowed well, and the group seemed to like it as much as any other group that size I have led. I feel great on the ride home: confident, calm, and very thankful that I pushed through my fears! This job has taken me much further out of my comfort zone than in the past, and it came out fine! What got me get so worked up? Maybe this is the cycle of growth. It seemed to take no time at all to get home. I love Laughter Yoga! I love being a Thriver!*

Wow! Adrienne did great! Don't you agree? Do try this at home yourself. See if you can drown out the Inner Critic with all the joy and confidence that doing something you love can bring you.

## THE EXERCISE: CONNECT WITH HAPPY PERSON INSIDE

Writing about what makes us happy brings us back to another exercise in the Seven Steps to Thriving After Abuse that I also think is worth revisiting here. The Happy Person Inside is your best cheerleader, and she loves you, loves you, loves you unconditionally! She has great wisdom to share with you. Make it big and bold!

**PROMPT:** Write a letter to yourself in your Thriver Zone Journal.

Dear (insert your name)

> *I Am the Happy Person Inside You and I Want to Tell You Something . . .*

WOW! Wasn't that great? Now read aloud what you have written. You need to get this wondrous, happy, strong, wise voice out into the Universe.

I bet what you wrote was very positive and very supportive of you and where you are now. Of course it was! The Happy Person Inside You thinks you are a fabulous person doing fabulous things! She is there for you always, no matter what.

She knows you so well because she is you, the best side of you – the thriver in you – and you want to maintain contact with her. We'll ask her later in this part of the book to help you envision a future for yourself and your children that is truly wonderful.

Here's a sample letter from a woman I have worked with.

### I AM THE HAPPY PERSON INSIDE
### and I want to tell you something . . .

*You have accomplished so much in your life. I am so proud of you. I want to tell you not to give up. There is greatness and great things that will come to you in the future. Remain patient. All your hard work has not gone unnoticed. Keep pressing forward and stay with God. He will never give up on you. He has carried you thus far. You're an inspiration; don't let your past dictate your future.*

*You've always dreamt of becoming a doctor, and you are well on your way. Don't let anyone or any obstacle hold you back. I will bring you plenty of business when you're ready. I know you're going to make it big. Keep smiling, honey, that beautiful smile of yours. And remember to never look back. You will never forget, but you can move forward. See those trials and tribulations as stepping-stones. I can't wait to see your name on the billboard. I'm already picking out my gown for graduation. I love you. It's time for you to shine, honey! You deserve it!*

*– TAWANDA*

Don't you just love it? When Tawanda first read this to me, I was blown away. If she puts all the positive energy (**Map Point A**) of her Happy Person Inside out there and uses it to push along her focused desire (See **Map Point B** which we'll be working on next) – like becoming a doctor – there is nothing Tawanda can't do!

Here's where we begin. First quiet the Inner Critic and keep her under wraps. Use affirmations every day, posted everywhere in your house, to do that. Explore what makes you happy and connect regularly with the Happy Person Inside. Ask for her advice; get her cheering you on.

**Map Point A – Getting Positive Energy** is a start on your Journey to the Real YOU!

✑**PROMPT:** Make a list on a separate page in your Thriver Zone Journal of the ways you will get and maintain your Positive Energy (Map Point A).

[NOTE: For each Map Point in this book, let's add to the same page so you fill in ***The Road Map to the Journey to the Real YOU!*™** as we go.]

**SAMPLE LIST for Getting Positive Energy –**

Do something that makes me happy

Take on the Inner Critic

Post my affirmations and recite them every morning

Stay connected with the Happy Person Inside every day.

~ ~ ~ ~ ~ ~ ~ ~ ~ ~ ~ ~ ~ ~

*We are all inventors, each sailing out on a voyage*
*of discovery, guided each by a private chart, of which*
*there is no duplicate. The world is all gates, all opportunities.*

— RALPH WALDO EMERSON

*What you think you become.*

*What you feel you attract.*

*What you imagine, you create.*

– BUDDHA

# Map Point B

## FOCUS YOUR DESIRES

*The starting point of all achievement is desire.*

— NAPOLEON HILL

## FOCUS YOUR DESIRES:

- **Think about what you want and why you want it. Focus your energy and emotions on getting it. Be positive and passionate about it.**

- **Remember, a desire for lots of money or material things can turn into an empty wish that doesn't lead to happiness. Your desires should take you to the things you love and the Real YOU.**

- **A desire for creative and emotional abundance can take you to a place of freedom and peace in a life of great purpose and compassion for humanity.**

*The size of your success is measured by*
*the strength of your desire.*

— ROBERT KIYOSAKI

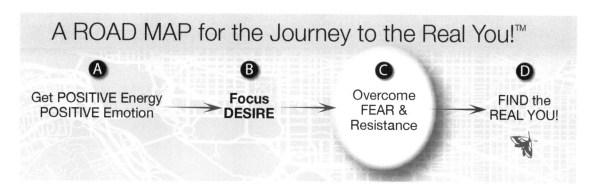

## MAP POINT B — Focus Your Desires

Each of us has some idea of what we want to do or accomplish in our lives. That desire can be as simple as wanting a new car or a new job – or as complex as world peace!

But often, as women who have been abused, we lose track of what we want. Over a period of time, an abusive person can wear us down and stand in the way of getting the job we've always wanted or the education we need to get us there. If you've ever had a desire to have peace in your home, the abuser's behavior can shatter that dream in a second!

Let's see if we can bring up some of our dreams and desires once again and take them out for a spin. Don't worry if you have never felt like you knew what you wanted to do with your life. We'll work on that too. It's all part of the next **Map Point B** on *The Road Map for the Journey to the Real YOU!™* – finding and focusing our desires so that they can come true.

## THE EXERCISE: WHAT WOULD YOU DO IF . . .

Ever wonder what you would do if you had no constraints and a lot of money? Write from this prompt in your Thriver Zone Journal and see what you desire.

✎ **PROMPT:** *If I had $10 million and all the time to do whatever I wanted, I'd . . .*

Over the years, I have asked hundreds of women that same question, and the answers have been humbling.

What if you had a lot of money – maybe a million or ten million? Or – what the heck! – what if you had billions and trillions of dollars, which is what the really wealthy people have to work with? What would you do? Most of women I've worked with say they would do something good and helpful to others with the money. Sure, they'd pay bills, buy houses for their children and other family members, but they would also start a nonprofit organization to serve those less fortunate or in abusive, dangerous situations. Then, too, travel, relaxing, and enjoying life comes up. So much to do! So little time!

Let me list some of the desires that usually come up with the women I have worked with who have experienced abuse. It includes things like:

**SAMPLE LIST:**

*Travel with my family*

*Buy a house*

*Pay off my bills*

*Go back to school*

*Start a business*

*Open a center for women and children*

While they can make a great list, many of these women I have worked with can't imagine that any of these desires will ever come true. Some tell me that it's impossible because they are too old . . . or too young; they don't have the money to achieve them, or they simply have no idea how to manifest their dreams. These desires seem beyond their reach, and they have no hope of things changing in the short or long-term.

Why is it that, though we can imagine wanting these things in our life and even write them down, we still have no real belief they can happen? They are indeed focused desires, they are specific, and for some people they are very doable. Why not for all of us? What keeps us from living the life of our dreams?

I believe the answer to that question lies in the fact that we all have some limiting beliefs about ourselves. These are thoughts about how we perceive our abilities or talents or how we think our past situations and circumstances hold us back from future happiness. Or we lack confidence in a vision for a life different from the one we have right now.

While we'll talk more about our fears and limiting beliefs about ourselves later in this book, for now here are some examples of limiting beliefs about ourselves:

- *There is no way I can create the life I want right now.*
- *My biggest fear is that I'll never get my life together.*
- *Bad things always seem to happen to me.*
- *I'll never figure out who I am or what I want to be when I grow up.*
- *I don't take any big risks.*

- *Life is too scary.*

- *Abuse has always been in my life. I can't do much about it.*

From this list of limiting beliefs, there are probably some that you always feel that way, some that you sometimes feel that way, and still others that you never feel that way. You might even notices that some may have shifted from always to sometimes or never from the past to now. If so, you have already been moving away from the limited view of yourself as a victim or survivor of what has happened to you, to the perspective of a thriver – more open, more positive and more alive!

Remember our definition of a thriver:

*A thriver is a happy, self-confident and productive individual who believes she has a prosperous life ahead of her. She is primed to follow her dreams, go back to school, find a new job, start her own business, or write her story. She believes in herself and in her future so much that she will not return to an abusive relationship. She speaks knowledgeably and confidently about her experiences and is not stuck in her anger or need for revenge.*

*Living well is her best revenge!*

Yes, a woman who is thriving is primed to follow her dreams and manifest her desires. So with all the positive energy you have available to you from **Map Point A,** let's now add our focused desires from **Map Point B.** Maybe the list you made with the $10-million writing prompt earlier in this book would be more of your long-term goals. Some of them might be short-term desires to get to a long-term goal.

For example, if you have a desire to get a better, higher paying job as a long-term goal, your short-term goal may be to go back to school so you can get better qualified for that job. Or if you have always dreamed of becoming a lawyer, doctor, or nurse, what would you have to do in the short-term to get you to those long-term goals? Probably finish your undergraduate studies, get loans to finance further education, and so on.

It's important to see here that every time you focus on a desire and push through any limiting beliefs about manifesting it, you will have more confidence and belief in yourself to take on the next desire, and the next, and the next! Soon all your goals will be met, and you will have all that you dreamed and even more!

Over the years, working with hundreds of women who have experienced abuse, we have started with that simple writing prompt, *If I had $10 million and all the time to do whatever I wanted, I'd…* The list they generated allowed them to see that what they dreamed of and what they desired was possible once they were on the journey to thriving. We'll have more about that later in this book, but for now, let's work a little more on focusing our desires, and then we'll move to how to get past our fear and limiting beliefs about ourselves.

Below are more prompts to get some desires focused. See what you can add to your list below by writing a little more about what you are passionate about.

✒ **PROMPT:** What did you want to be when you grew up?

Who were your heroes growing up or now?

What did they do that you wanted to do?

What did you love to do as a little girl?

What are you passionate about today?

What opportunities do you see in what happened to you in the past?

How could you help others because of what you have experienced?

What do you love to do today? What comes easily for you?

Great! Now look at what you have written from these prompts in your Thriver Zone Journal. You should be able to identify a few focused desires there. But before we go on next Map Point to see how we can overcome any obstacles you may see to getting there, I wanted to do another exercise that puts you in a better, less resistant frame of mind about achieving all that you desire.

## THE EXERCISE: CREATE ABUNDANCE

One of the things I have learned to ask for in my life is not necessarily for weath and all of its pitfalls, but for abundance. Abundance is more than just having a lot of money – it is an emotional state of mind that lets you see so many things in your life as coming from a place of plenty and prosperity for which you can be grateful.

**PROMPT:** Write words that describe what abundance means for you.

**SAMPLE LIST**
**ABUNDANCE IS . . .**

Freedom, Passion, Peace, Faith, Home, Mobility, Love, Security,

Good Job, Good Health, Good Times, Stability, Giving Back to Others,

Family, Friends, Connection, Full, Glow, Self-Love

Now let's create some affirmations that can bring abundance in our lives!

**PROMPT:** Write abundance affirmations in your Thriver Zone Journal.

**SAMPLE LIST!**
**MY ABUNDANCE AFFIRMATIONS ARE . . .**

I am open and ready to attract abundance in my life.

I release any negative feelings about money.

I am focused on prosperity and opportunity.

I am wealthy beyond measure.

I live a full and fulfilling life!

I am prosperous, generous and kind.

My heart is full.

I have more love and contentment than I ever imagined.

I understand my purpose, and I open my heart for good.

I am courageous, wild, and free!

I am a thriver!

Wow! With that frame of mind, you are quickly moving forward to matching your focused desires to the Real YOU and finding your power and purpose in life. By closely aligning your desires with the Real YOU, manifesting your desires will be even more possible, and you will push through your fears and limiting beliefs more successfully.

✍ **PROMPT:** On the same page in your Thriver Zone Journal where you recorded **Map Point A,** write down some of your focused desires that you want to manifest from **Map Point B.**

**SAMPLE LIST – My Focused Desires**

Go to medical school

Finish college

Get my GED

Get a job helping other women like me

Go back to school to get training

Volunteer in organizations to find my passion

Write with gratitude about my abundant life every day

~ ~ ~ ~ ~ ~ ~ ~ ~ ~ ~ ~ ~ ~ ~

*Within all of us is a divine capacity to manifest and attract all that we need and desire.*

— WAYNE DYER

*You gain strength, courage,
and confidence by every
experience in which you really
stop to look fear in the face.
You must do the thing which
you think you cannot do.*

— ELEANOR ROOSEVELT

# Map Point C

## OVERCOME YOUR FEARS

*Love is what we were born with.*

*Fear is what we have learned here.*

— MARIANNE WILLIAMSON

## OVERCOME YOUR FEARS AND TAKE THE RISK:

- With high energy and strong, positive emotions you can push past your fears and resistance to the Real YOU.

- This kind of energy and emotion makes you feel passionate about what you desire and work even harder to overcome your fears.

*The size of your success is measured by*

*the strength of your desire.*

— ROBERT KIYOSAKI

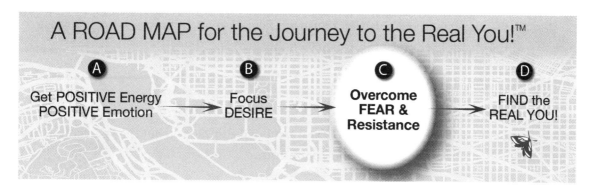

A ROAD MAP for the Journey to the Real You!™

A — Get POSITIVE Energy POSITIVE Emotion

B — Focus DESIRE

C — Overcome FEAR & Resistance

D — FIND the REAL YOU!

## MAP POINT C — Overcome Your Fears, Take the Risk

There is no question about it – fear can block us from making our dreams come true. Fear of failure, fear of rejection or even fear of success can limit our beliefs about ourselves and keep us from taking the risk of finding out who we really are and what will make us happy. We have already dealt with such "limiting beliefs" about ourselves when we took on the Inner Critic in the previous Map Point A.

Remember how good it felt when we wrote positive responses and affirmations to negative thoughts like "I don't deserve to be happy," "You'll never amount to anything," and "You are a loser."

With the strong, positive energy we experienced in **MAP Point A,** and the focusing of our desires in MAP Point B, we'll have all the momentum we need to push past our fears in **MAP Point C** and find the Real YOU at **MAP Point D.**

# THE EXERCISE: CHALLENGE LIMITING BELIEFS

Let's go back to the affirmations you created in the **Map Point A** that helped you quiet the Inner Critic and bring up your positive energy. Here we'll use similar affirmations to make you feel positive about yourself and passionate about what you desire so you can push through your fears on this part of the journey to the "Real YOU."

Let's start with the list of limiting beliefs from our last **Map Point B** that particularly resonated for you. See you If can think of others that might be influencing you.

✎ **PROMPT:** Create two columns on a page in your Thriver Zone Journal and write your limiting beliefs in the left-hand column.

Now in the right-hand column add a strong affirmation or unlimited belief response to each one of the statements in your left-hand column.

Be bold! Think big and be outrageous!

What is your highest, best thought to push you to a positive place? You don't even have to believe what you write – at least not right now. But I'd like to see you put the vision out there of unlimited possibilities for yourself and your future.

# TOP TEN FEARS IN LIFE

**FEAR OF...**

1. ABANDONMENT — I'm afraid that someone will leave me, and I'll feel alone and vulnerable. This makes me feel unloved and unlovable.

2. REJECTION — I'm afraid that someone will tell me to go away, and I'll feel bad. This could happen in the workplace, or in a relationship.

3. FAILURE — I'm afraid that I'll fail again like I have in the past.

4. SUCCESS — I'm afraid I might do something right, and the struggle will be over. What will I do then? I fear it will all be taken away from me.

5. BETRAYAL — I'm afraid someone will be unfaithful or disloyal to me. To avoid that, I let someone else define who I am or set limits on me.

6. LONELINESS — I'm afraid I'll be alone and feel lonesome. Can I learn to be alone without feeling lonely and spend quality time with myself?

7. ILLNESS — I'm afraid I'll get sick and I won't be able to do something that could make me happy or move my life forward.

8. AGING — I'm afraid I'm too old to start over, or to be taken seriously. I need to learn that I don't have to act my age or be defined by it.

9. LOSS — I have lost so much in my life. I'm afraid I'll lose more.

10. DEATH — I'm afraid that when I die I will cease to exist. Doesn't our spirit transcend death? If so, then our birth is harder than our death!

Here's a sample:

| LIMITING BELIEF | UNLIMITED BELIEF |
|---|---|
| There is no way I can create the life I want right now. | I can be anything I want to be! |
| My biggest fear is that I'll never get my life together. | I push through my fears every day! |
| I'll never figure out what I want to be when I'm grown up. | I am making an amazing life for myself. |
| I don't take any big risks. | I'm taking a risk on me! |
| Life is too scary. | I am fearless and following my passions! |

Can you see how your limiting beliefs about yourself can create a wall of resistance and block you from manifesting your desires? If you don't believe you can do it, it won't happen! You must begin to break down that resistance, which in my experience, has fear at its base.

Fear? What kind of fears do we have?

When you looked at the list on the previous page, TOP TEN FEARS IN LIFE, did you notice something? All these fears are thoughts, not things!

For example, we have a fear of being rejected. That fear is probably based on a previous experience when we were rejected, and now our fear is a thought that we might be rejected again. Because of that thought, we may not take an action in the future based on our fear from a past situation. But if we change that present thought, we may be able to take the present action without fear. For example, I might not go after the new job I really want because I'm afraid I will be rejected for that job the way I have been rejected for a job in the past. I can remember how it felt to be rejected, and I don't want to feel like that again, so I won't even try for the new position.

NOTE: Physical fear is different. That is not just a thought, it is a thing. If you have a fear that someone will harm you physically, particularly based on a previous experience with that person, you will have a harder – but not impossible – task to push through that fear. But if you can push through a fear of being physically in danger – such as leaving a physically abusive relationship – you can do about anything! That's an amazing accomplishment and a bench-mark for you in the future!

It is important to realize how our fearful thoughts can easily turn into limited beliefs about ourselves. See below how these fears match up to some limiting beliefs.

| Example of Fear-Based Beliefs | Positive Responses |
|---|---|
| *Fear of failure:* | |
| I will never get my life together. | My life is unfolding perfectly. |
| *Fear of success:* | |
| Whatever I might accomplish, it will be taken away from me. | I celebrate my successes. Each one has a lasting impact on my life. |
| *Fear of loneliness:* | |
| I am incomplete without someone else. | I love who I am! No one else defines me. |
| *Fear of rejection:* | |
| I have suffered too much. | I am unique and special. |
| I'll never get over it. | I am moving on with my life. |
| | I look forward to the great things ahead. |

Wow! Those fearful thoughts get even more forbidding when combined with limiting beliefs. Let's keep our positive responses ready as we move later in the book into manifesting the focused desires we've identified at **Map Point B.**

You can also turn your positive responses into affirmations like the ones you created earlier in this book. Write them on pieces of paper and post them about your house – on the bathroom mirror or on your computer monitor so you can see them every day and absorb them. Have them ready to use when things get moving and you feel a fearful thought coming on!

All right! Now that we have shifted our limited beliefs and fears into unlimited potential and positive energy, let's write about vanquishing our fear.

## THE EXERCISE: IF I HAD NO FEAR . . .

✎ **PROMPT:** Write from "If I had no fear (no limiting beliefs), I would . . ."

*REMEMBER!* You have no fears. Nothing is holding you back now! Go for it!

*MAKE THIS BIG!* It can be a list of things you would do or a description of how you would feel with no fear. You might want to listen to some soothing music before and as you write from this prompt.

Here's a few writing samples on this prompt by the women I have worked with:

**IF I HAD NO FEAR . . .**

> *. . . I would feel limitless, like I was always flying. Like nothing could hold me back, like no negative thoughts or words from others could stick to me, or prevent my smiling and my joy. I would follow my dreams, my inspirations, and the voice of God in each moment directing me to do the right thing, the best thing.*
>
> *– CATHRYN*

> *. . . I would dance to every song I hear. I would sing to each song that is played on the radio. I would smile and laugh and not worry what others thought of me. I would jump out of bed and go shopping with my hair sticking up. I wouldn't care if I was chunky. I wouldn't care if I cried at a movie and people saw me. I would go back to stopping and saying hello to everyone I meet. I would make my goal list and finish each goal within my set time. I would be spontaneous and not plan things. I would skip down the grocery store aisles and give smiles to the clerks who ring me out. I would talk with people at the diner just to say hi. I would give a little extra to the stores just in case they had people who didn't have enough for their groceries. I would look for a four-leaf clover.*
>
> *– HOLLY*

> *. . . I could get on that plane and see other countries. Or I'd take a train to New York City and ice skate at Rockefeller Center when the Christmas tree is lit up there. I would have no fear of looking over the falls at Niagara Falls or riding up and down the elevator in any building. I would try out for a part in a movie, maybe a Steven Spielberg film or a comedy with Robin Williams. I'd even ask for their autograph. I'd give the best interview and get a great job! I wouldn't care what other people thought of me. I'd finish learning how to play the keyboard, guitar, and harmonica. I'd play one of those instruments in a band someday. Sing a song before a crowd. WOW!*
>
> *– CHRISTINE*

> *. . . I would follow every dream that I have! I would not fear being too tired or not having enough money. I would feel SO FREE to do what I want to do without any*

*second-guessing myself. I would go back to school and get my degree in counseling and open a center to help other men and women and provide for them whatever they needed. I would help the abused and meet their needs no matter what they were so that all women and men could heal. That healing would cause the ripple effect and move out to others who need to be healed.*

*– JO-ANN*

Wow! What a great list of things we could all do if we had no fear! We can step outside our comfort zones and find a space where we have no bad feelings or experiences to hold us back. Past events and situations can keep us chained to the fears of our past, and we can't always see those events and situations through a different lens even if we are in a healthier place now and may feel more healed. For example, we may look at difficult or traumatic events more often with feelings that can bring up negative thoughts to inflame our fears instead of exploring more positive, productive thoughts and emotions that can break down our resistance and move our lives forward.

What other difficult emotions besides fear can be engendered from past situations that might build up your resistance to change or moving on? What can you do to shift those feelings from negative to positive? Below is a suggestion.

## THE EXERCISE: CHOOSE GUILT, BLAME, OR APPRECIATION

This is a great exercise that can allow you to work through your feelings about things that have happened to you in the past that still carry a lot of negative emotions for you. You can turn those feelings, based on guilt and blame, into more positive ones, like appreciation. You can see the sample writing below to help you with this writing prompt.

✍ **PROMPT:** Write about an event in your life and how you feel about it.

*What event?*

*What feelings of guilt do you have?*

*What feelings of blame? (of yourself or others)*

*What feelings of appreciation?*

Here's a sample of how to write about an event from these three perspectives – Guilt, Blame, Appreciation:

## *Event:* What My Children Witnessed When I was in an Abusive Relationship

*Guilt:* I feel guilty about what the abuse in my life has done to my children. I have exposed them to danger, let them see me as a victim, and I may have taught them to be victims too.

*Blame:* It's all my fault. I should have left earlier. I should have seen it sooner. I blame him for not being able to change. I thought he would. It's my mother's fault. She taught me to be a victim in her own marriage. My father was an abuser. He's to blame for all the grief in my life.

*Appreciation:* Thank God, I got out when I did. My children are stronger because they know about life's struggles and they have seen how I acted to break the cycle of violence in our lives. I am proud of myself and my children. Each day we celebrate our violence-free lives, safe and free from harm! Our lives are getting better every day. We are thriving!

Can you see and feel how in the sample above the energy shifted when the writing moved from negative thoughts of guilt and blame to the positive ones of appreciation? It is a welcome shift that makes you ask, "Which energy do I want to have in my life?" We can't always change things that have happened to us, but we can change how we react to and think about them. It is a welcome shift!

Now look at what you wrote. Can you feel the same shift in energy? How might you resolve some of those feelings of guilt and blame you have from past events? How could you let them go?

Write some affirmations you can repeat daily that might shake off these negative feelings and move you to a different frame of mind about difficulties from your past. Here's some that I use regularly:

- All things happen for a reason.
- It was NOT my fault.
- I am grateful for the life I lead now.
- Today I am in a positive mind-set that allows my energy to flow.
- I forgive those who have harmed me and peacefully detach from them.

That last affirmation is always a challenging one for me. It's hard to detach from what other people have done to us; it's easier to wallow in the pain of betrayal and resentment. Yet granting forgiveness to others for what they did to harm us is nothing compared to having to forgive ourselves.

Forgiveness! That's a word most victims want to avoid. Do we have to forgive those who have harmed us? What's the use of that? Maybe we should take a look at that . . .

## THE EXERCISE: FORGIVE YOURSELF

One of the most difficult questions my family was asked after my niece Maggie's death was whether we had or could ever forgive the ex-boyfriend who killed her. My initial reaction to the question was that, while I might choose to forgive him, I'll never forget what he did. The pain he has caused will affect me the rest of my life. Now I find that this question really begs another, more gut-wrenching one: "Will I ever forgive myself for what happened to Maggie?" Now that is a question!

One afternoon when I was working with some of the women in my Thriver community, we stumbled upon this issue of forgiveness. One of the women in the group was talking about how she was still having a hard time dealing with the man who abused her, now her ex-husband. He was the father of her two children, one of whom was in serious emotional and psychological pain as a result of what he witnessed as a child in his parents' marriage. He was under the watchful eye of therapists, child welfare workers – not to mention judges, lawyers, and so many other "helping professionals."

Her anguish was that, after all this time, no one (except her) was getting that her children's father was as abusive and manipulative to her and the children in the long, drawn-out post-divorce process as he had been to them in their marriage. Why was she the one that had to keep on fighting him? Why couldn't the others see him for what he was and help her before he destroyed her children?

While there were many ways we could have talked about all the issues and feelings she was bringing up, I encouraged her to look at the way she was seeing her reality. Was it really that all was lost and she would never get this man and his abuse out of her life? Or could she see that, in reality, she was making progress? She was out of the marriage, and she had gotten others involved in the on-going struggle she had been having with her ex-husband about her son. At least one of the professionals had seen and experienced her ex-husband's anger and had confessed to her that she was afraid to go to his home unaccompanied by another worker for fear of what this man might do.

Was she really supposed to forgive this man? His abuse never stops!

Then I asked her the BIG question: "Have you ever forgiven yourself for getting hooked up with this man in the first place?"

That was the showstopper. With tears streaming down her face and the words choking in her throat, she said, "No, I can't forgive myself for any of it. It is all my fault. The thing is, he does provoke me. I lose it even when we are in family therapy. I'm hurting my children."

I looked around the room and saw in every woman's face that they too had faced those same feelings and doubts. In fact, none of us had forgiven ourselves for anything. And so, our assignment for the afternoon was born.

You can do it now. Think of all the ways you blame or shame yourself for the abuse and its impact on you, your life, and maybe your children's lives. Let's write from the following prompt.

> **PROMPT:** "I am not responsible for the abuse. I forgive myself for . . ."

The power of forgiveness is immeasurable, and if we can forgive ourselves, think how powerful it would be and how it could move us forward with our lives and help us to thrive!

It can certainly bring us beyond our fears, resistance, and limiting beliefs about ourselves and change the trajectory of our lives.

In my process of forgiving myself, I have learned some things about the journey beyond the pain and shock of Maggie's death. These two have been the biggest for me:

- **Learn to love the chaos, the struggle, the process.** If you could figure it all out now, it would never be quite as wonderful as it will be if you just let it happen.
  *Have patience with everything unresolved in your heart and try to love the questions themselves. Live the questions now. Perhaps then, someday far in the future, you will gradually, without ever noticing it, live your way into the answer.*
  –Rainer Marie Rilke, *Letters to a Poet*

- **Fear may be our biggest and only obstacle to living our dreams.** That fear is usually not physical fears, but thoughts and limited beliefs about ourselves that keep us from doing what we desire.

  *You gain strength, courage and confidence by every experience in which you really stop to look fear in the face. You must do the thing you think you cannot do.*
  – Eleanor Roosevelt

✎ **PROMPT:** On the same page in your Thriver Zone Journal where you recorded **Map Point A and B,** write down some techniques you will use to overcome your fears and limiting beliefs in this **Map Point C.**

**SAMPLE LIST – Overcome Fears**

Challenge limited beliefs

Switch from guilt and blame to appreciation

Use affirmations to move my thoughts from fearful to more positive ones.

Review my If I Had No Fear list regularly and add to it if I like.

Forgive myself; find opportunity in loss

~ ~ ~ ~ ~ ~ ~ ~ ~ ~ ~ ~ ~ ~

*Where the fear has gone there will be nothing.*
*Only I will remain.*

— FRANK HERBERT

Let the beauty of

what you love

be what you do.

– RUMI

# Map Point D

## FIND THE REAL <u>YOU</u>

*Seek out that which makes you feel most deeply and vitally alive*
*. . . the inner voice which says, "This is the real me."*
— WILLIAM JAMES

## WHAT THE *REAL YOU* WANTS FOR YOU:

- To thrive in a happy, satisfying life, free of fear.

- To become the person you were meant to be.

- To find joy, peace, bliss, freedom, abundance, and prosperity.

- To live a life of purpose based on what is important to you.

- To reclaim your power, find out who you are and want to be.

*The privilege of a lifetime is being who you are.*
— JOSEPH CAMPBELL

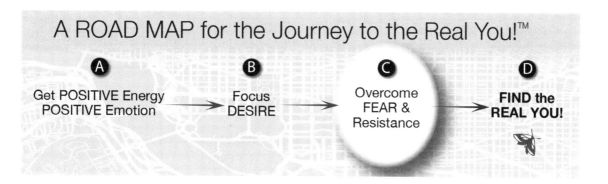

## MAP POINT D — Find the Real YOU

Wouldn't it be amazing if when you did something good – particularly when you had to overcome your worse fears – you'd get a big reward?

Surprise! You do get a prize, and it's a good one!

In reaching the last **Map Point D,** finding the Real YOU is your reward for taking the journey beyond abuse and manifesting a new life of power and purpose!

The Real YOU is the part of us that is immortal and cannot die. It is our spirit, soul, or the divine – whatever word you might use to describe it, however inadequately. Sometimes I call it my Happy Person Inside, the part of me that has been untouched by all the hard, difficult, bad stuff that has happened to me in this lifetime.

(See the exercise on Connecting with the Happy Person Inside earlier
in this book with **Map Point A, Get Positive Energy.**)

My Real YOU is pure ecstasy, and when I'm there, I can feel its power and majesty. I feel most deeply and vitally alive!

Does all that sound impossible or too unrealistic to you? It shouldn't. In fact, it is indeed a very natural, human process to be in touch with our most authentic selves. You may have been in touch with that part of you before and didn't know it. Or you didn't have same words for the experience as I do.

But think about it! Every time you go for what makes you feel happy, content, and fulfilled, your Real YOU (or the Happy Person Inside) is coming through. It's the Thriver energy that makes us feel like more than just surviving all that has happened to us in this lifetime. It's that moment when it all makes sense, or it feels good that we took the journey and got to the other side. Here's some of the words we might use to describe now it feels to connect with the Real YOU –

**Beautiful, Radiant, Glowing, Loving**
**Deserving, Beloved, Cherished, Unconditional Love**
**Caring, Wonderful, Smart, Graceful**
**Free, Powerful, Good, Strong**
**Happy, Creative, Pure Joy, Found Paradise**

## WHAT IS IMPORTANT TO YOU?

From the list below, choose the things that are most important to you in your life and work.

*RANK THEM AS:*   *#1 — Most Important — Absolutely Must Have*

*#2 — Less Important — Nice to Have*

*#3 — Least Important — Don't Need*

___ ☼   Making the World More Beautiful

___ ☼   Accomplishing Something

___ ☼   Having a Good Balance Between Work and Play

___ ☼   Being Liked

___ ☼   Getting Ahead in My Career

___ ☼   Working Well with My Coworkers

___ ☼   Having Good Friends

___ ☼   Being Creative

___ ☼   Doing Meaningful Work

___ ☼   Making a Difference

___ ☼   Doing Good Work, Excellence

___ ☼   Having Low Stress

___ ☼   Having Power

___ ☼   Helping or Healing Others

___ ☼   Having Integrity, Always Doing the Right Thing

___ ☼   A Good Salary

___ ☼   Making Sure My Children Are Well Prepared for Life

___ ☼   Finding What Will Make Me Happy

___ ☼   Being Independent

___ ☼   Being Intellectually Challenged in My Work

___ ☼   Learning New Things, Adding New Skills

___ ☼   Having a Pleasant Work Environment

___ ☼   Having a Lot of Status, Prestige

___ ☼   Being Recognized and Valued for What I Do by My Boss and Coworkers

___ ☼   Having Financial Security

___ ☼   Feeling Good About Myself and My Life

___ ☼   Providing for Myself and My Children

___ ☼   Taking Care of Myself

___ ☼   Having a Good Family Life

We like how it feels to be in the Real YOU. It's warm and fuzzy and full of love. Because it feels so good to be in the Real YOU, we as human beings seek out and long for things that our Real YOU values. What are those values? That's hard to say because they are different for each one of us.

For me, my Real YOU seeks out meaningful work and ways to help and heal others. I also want to accomplish something and have integrity in my work.

What is important to your Real YOU? Not sure? Let's take the survey on the previous page so you can see what is of value and importance to your Real YOU!

## THE EXERCISE: CHOOSE WHAT'S IMPORTANT TO YOU

Take a look at the items that you ranked as #1 on the list of what is most important to you. (If you have more than three items marked #1, see if you can narrow it down to your top three or less.)

✎**PROMPT:** Write down your top three #1 items from the survey. Then write your top #2 and #3 choice. Write about what those choices mean for you. What do they say about your Real YOU's values and priorities? Make this fun and exciting! You're exploring a whole new part of YOU!

For example, say you had the following items listed as your top #1s:

***Accomplishing Something • Doing Meaningful Work • Helping or Healing Others***

– I would say that your Real YOU will celebrate you finding a caring community and meaningful work that helps and serves others.

If your list looked more like this:

***Having a Good Balance between Work and Play • Making Sure My Children Are Well Prepared for Life • Having a Good Family Life***

– I would say that your Real YOU is invested in having family and friends that teach and practice unconditional love.

Finally, if your list included:

**Doing Good Work, Excellence • Making a Difference • Having Integrity, Always Doing the Right Thing**

> – Integrity and Excellence excites your Real YOU.

What you also can get from this exercise is what the Real YOU is not interested in. Here's an example:

If you put these items as #3:

**Getting Ahead in My Career • Having a Lot of Status and Prestige • Having Financial Security • Having Power • Being Liked**

> – I'd say you are a person who is interested in more than financial success, gaining power, or getting ahead just to get ahead. But maybe that's not your Real YOU.

Most women I have worked with who have been abused or controlled in their lives will pick one or more of these items as a #3. In some cases, a woman who has been in an abusive, controlling relationship is least likely to be interested in having power or measuring her success by external factors, such as how much money or status she has.

On the other hand, I have also had women pick "Having Power" as a #2 or even a #1 item because, for the first time in their lives, they have the sense that they are finally coming into their power. Those women are most likely to have also chosen as a #1 or #2 "Being Independent," "Finding What Makes Me Happy," or "Feeling Good About Myself and My Life."

Let's look at the words that best describe the Real YOU in all of us.

**Fearless, Focused, Expressive, Compassionate**
**Creative, Adventurous, Loving, Playful, Silly**
**Independent, Resilient, Connected**
**Courageous, Persistent, Intuitive**
**Comforting, Fun-Loving, Free**

Now let's add some of the words you may have chosen from the last few exercises we have done, including What Is Most Important to You.

For example, words like these might fit for you:

**Integrated, Meaningful Work**
**Balanced Life, Feel My Worthiness**
**Helping, Healing Others, Make Choices**
**Connected to Inner Wisdom, Intuition, Abundance**

Now that you can feel Real YOU and have some idea of what she is about, you are ready to take on the next challenge of this book.

What we need to do now, having followed all map points on *The Road Map for the Journey to the Real YOU!*™ is create a new life for ourselves and our loved ones.

## PURSUE A LIFE OF POWER AND PURPOSE

I've done it, and you can too! I never dreamed that I would be writing books like this one and others. Yet I have been a writer all my life and had always wanted to be published.

Once I got positive energy, focused my desire on writing a book, pushed through my fears, and recognized that this desire matched my Real YOU's value of doing meaningful work and helping and healing others, my book became a reality!

You can have dreams and desires come true too. Fueled by positive energy (**Map Point A**) with focused desires (**Map Point B**), you can push through your fears and limiting beliefs about yourself (**Map Point C**) and find the Real YOU (**Map Point D**), ready to create a life of power and for a life of power and purpose!

You can build your new life – even after abuse, violence, trauma, disappointment, and betrayal. How empowering will that be! And you're going to make the most of it! You will dream big and take risks you never thought possible.

Once there, you can truly embrace the idea that "living well is the best revenge!" Whatever happened to you in the past and whoever did it to you, what those people who hurt you didn't want was for you to live well! In their attempt to control, humiliate, and destroy you, the one thing that will really get them is the thought that, without them in your life, you will do well.

Remember! You are the one who is going to grow and change and prosper. Those who have abused, hurt, betrayed, and disappointed you probably will not. I know this because

I've worked with many women who have been abused, and I have watched their lives change forever when they have connected with the Real YOU inside them on their journey to thriving. But generally, their former partners' lives have stayed about the same. In fact, some others simply have moved on only to find someone else they could treat as badly. Most may never make real changes for the better in their lives.

So that is our revenge! We are living well, and they are not! It's as simple as that.

Let's get on with the rest of your sweet, wonderful life!

✍ **PROMPT:** On the same page in your Thriver Zone Journal where you recorded **Map Point A, B, C,** write down some techniques you will use to find the Real YOU.

### SAMPLE LIST – Find the Real YOU

Review my list what is important to my Real YOU often.

Write Affirmations for my Real YOU – such as "I am Powerful, Fearless, and Free!'

Post them around my house so I absorb them completely

Write regularly in my Thriver Zone Journal to and from the Real YOU

~ ~ ~ ~ ~ ~ ~ ~ ~ ~ ~ ~ ~ ~

*What lies behind us and what lies before us*
*are tiny matters compared to what lies within us.*

— RALPH WALDO EMERSON

*Trust in dreams, for in them*

*is hidden the gate to eternity.*

– Khalil Gibran

# Manifest Your Desires

## ALL THAT YOU DREAM CAN COME TRUE

*That which we manifest is before us;*
*we are the creators of our own destiny.*
— GARTH STEIN

*Never let life impede on your ability to manifest your dreams.*
*Dig deeper into your dreams and deeper into yourself and believe that*
*anything is possible, and make it happen.*
— CORIN NEMEC

### THE ART OF MANIFESTING YOUR DREAMS

Manifesting your desires – making your dreams come true – is the essence of the journey to the Real YOU. With each of the four Map Points which make up ***The Road Map for the Journey to the Real YOU!™***, I hope you have learned how simple but intense this journey can be.

Oddly enough, the word manifest in our language is used to describe some pretty intense experiences. Let's look again at the quotes about manifesting from people from various spheres in our society including martial arts, spirituality, and politics. All of them have used the word to signify a transcendent experience, something that takes us beyond the human realm into the more divine or sublime.

- *You are here to manifest your innate enlightenment.*

  – Morihei Ueshiba, a martial artist, founder of Japanese art of aikido

- *We were born to manifest the glory of God that is within us.*

  – Marianne Williamson, a spiritual leader in A Course in Miracles

- *Life is about, every single day, getting up to manifest your truth.*

  – Cory Booker, U.S. Senator from New Jersey

In any process that involves what we call the Real YOU or the Happy Person Inside, there will be a feeling of exhilaration, ecstasy, and pure joy when we have accomplished goals that transform our lives. I've seen it happen with many of women I've helped over the years take the journey from victim to survivor to thriver. They have manifested desires they thought would never be possible for them.

Why is the journey so transformational? The first part of my working definition of a thriver does say:

**A thriver is a happy, self-confident, and productive individual who believes she has a prosperous life ahead of her.**

So how does she get to that prosperous life ahead of her after perhaps a lifetime of being a victim or merely a survivor? I believe, from my own experiences and from observing these courageous women who have taken the journey beyond abuse, that we get there by first Entering the Thriver Zone and then by Staying in the Thriver Zone so we can manifest our desires and build, piece by piece, a new life that matches the values and passions of our Real YOU. That is truly a life of power and purpose!

## MANIFEST A LIFE OF POWER AND PURPOSE

Let's start by reviewing step-by-step the motivational model I have developed – **The Road Map for the Journey to the Real YOU!™** – laid out in the first part of this book.

Follow along through the four map points. It is your map now, so use it!

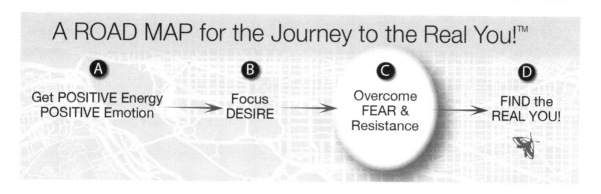

## MAP POINT A — Get Positive Energy

You begin your journey to the Real YOU by inviting pure, positive energy into your life. You see yourself as a thriver, not just a survivor, of abuse. You are no longer a victim — hopeless, helpless, and alone. Remember the definition of thriver:

*A thriver is a happy, self-confident and productive individual who believes she has a prosperous life ahead of her. She is primed to follow her dreams, go back to school, find a new job, start her own business, or write her story. She believes in herself and in her future so much that she will not return to an abusive relationship. She speaks knowledgeably and confidently about her experiences and is not stuck in her anger or need for revenge.*

*Living well is her best revenge!*

When you choose to go with your positive thoughts, not negative ones, you can propel yourself forward on your journey to the Real YOU and keep your life moving forward.

## MAP POINT B — Focus Your Desires

At this Map Point, you bring out your dreams and long-held desires and take them out for a spin! Don't worry if you don't know right now exactly what you want to do with your life. You are in abundance! Nothing is out of your grasp. If you are clear, hopeful, and inspired at this point of the journey, you can focus your desires and make your dreams can come true.

## MAP POINT C — Overcome Your Fears

Fear is a crippling thing! It can bring on anxiety and despair which can block you from moving beyond abuse. Fear of failure, fear of rejection, or even fear of success can limit your beliefs about yourself and keep you from taking the risk of finding out who you really are and what will make you happy. But here you are pushing through your fears and limiting beliefs, knocking down the barriers to connecting with the Real YOU! You have all the momentum to get there.

## MAP POINT D — Find the Real YOU

You've done it! Congratulations! You have reached the Real YOU – your Happy Ending. Your reward is that amazing feeling of being in contact with the spiritual, immortal part of you, the Real YOU. Being there makes you feel happy, content, and fulfilled. This euphoric feeling of being in the Real YOU give you even more positive energy to fuel your next focused desire.

For example, after successful manifesting your first desire to go back to school and celebrating graduation with the sweet, wonderful feeling of connecting with the Real YOU, you now use that powerfully good feeling of accomplishment to give you the positive energy to work on your next focused desire: get a great job in your new field.

## THE MOTIVATIONAL MODEL WORKS

After successfully using this model myself, I am now able to teach it to women who have experienced abuse, and they also have had success with it. How successful? You can judge that for yourself with the stories of manifesting below from a number of women I have worked with. Some have been with me for a number of years; others have come more recently into the Thriver community. Yet no matter how long they have been on the journey, they all have a story to tell.

## MEETING OPRAH

One of the more amazing manifesting stories comes from Sophia and her lifelong quest to meet Oprah Winfrey. A few years ago, I did a weekend retreat for the women in our Thriver community at a beachside retreat center on the Long Island Sound. We were definitely in the

Oprah energy that weekend. As the wind howled and the rain fell around us, nature's energy matched our own as we worked on focusing our intentions and visioning that all of our wild, wonderful dreams would come true.

We put together visions boards – collages of pictures and words that included our intentions and how we'd get support to accomplish them. The most important word we used was how we'd manifest them. All the vision boards included a picture of Oprah, and above mine I pasted a phrase from *O, The Oprah Magazine:* "Here We Go!"

That weekend we celebrated Oprah, not just as a very famous woman talk show host, but also as a prime example of what it is to be a THRIVER in one's life. A survivor of child sexual assault, Oprah's life journey paralleled so many of ours – from VICTIM TO SURVIVOR TO THRIVER!

We danced around that Saturday afternoon, each of us in turn pretending that we were on the Oprah show and presenting to her, as if in the future, how the intentions on our vision boards manifested and came true. Several of us played Oprah, wearing the Oprah crown that we made on Friday night with her picture on the front and words that epitomized her energy decorating it: courage, compassion, power, and dreamer.

One of us was particularly good at being Oprah, and that was Sophia. She inhabited the role of Oprah, showing exuberance, passion, and a sense of how when you work together with others, you can change the world. She was fabulous!

----

**The more you praise and celebrate your life,
the more there is to praise.** – *Oprah Winfrey*

----

That's why I wasn't surprised when I got a very excited phone message about five months later from Sophia. She had entered the "LIVE YOUR BEST LIFE EVER Spa Week" contest on the Oprah website and had gotten a call that she had won! That March she joined Oprah Winfrey and Gayle King at a famous spa in Arizona with all her expenses paid! We were ecstatic for Sophia. She had worked so hard and done so much to inspire all of us. But that week at the spa with Oprah and Gayle was only the beginning of the adventure.

Here's what Sophia wrote about it several years later:

*I am grateful for my LIVE YOUR BEST LIFE EVER experience. When I arrived at the spa, I could not swim. I was open to learning how to swim there, and that experience aired on national television. But when I returned home, I was still paralyzed by my fear from nearly drowning in high school and being molested as a child in the water.*

*Today with the help of God and many women friends in my life, I have triumphed over my fears. I started taking swimming lessons with teachers who help those who have a fear of water, and I finally swam across the pool. Last year I jumped into the Long Island Sound with women friends at a weekend retreat. Today, I AM A SWIMMER! I have also left a marriage clouded by domestic violence that could have put me on the eleven o'clock news. I am free of thirty-two years of strangleholds that had crippled me mentally, spiritually, and physically. Today, I am an advocate for women, helping them take the journey from VICTIM TO SURVIVOR TO THRIVER!*

*– SOPHIA*

Wow! Sophia's story is a great example of how to manifest something that you thought you couldn't do. Now it is your turn to write a story about manifesting. Think about something you thought you couldn't do. Maybe it was just last week or a few years ago or even something that happened to you as a kid. Write about it, using the prompts below and the outline I have given you. You can do this!

## THE EXERCISE: MANIFESTING – A FAIRY TALE!

✍ **PROMPT:** Write about something you thought you couldn't do, but you did.

How did you do that? What worked and didn't work?

How did it feel when you got through it?

What did you learn?

But I want you to frame the story as if it were a fairy tale. I called it "Manifesting – A Fairy Tale!" and I have included a template for you to follow.

# Manifesting– A Fairy Tale!

Make a list of things that you have done – big or small – that you thought you couldn't do, but you did! Pick one. Think of how you manifested that result. WRITE A STORY using prompts below. Have fun! Celebrate your success!

_____

ONCE UPON A TIME there was a girl who thought she couldn't . . .

She tried to . . .

And then she tried . . .

And she tried again . . .


There were negative voices in her head telling her . . .


But she decided not to listen. Instead positive voices told her . . .


In the end, she felt . . . (e.g., joy, strong, confident . . .)


She knew she felt her power when she . . .


Her experience taught her . . . the lessons learned . . .


With her success, she learned more about her purpose in life which is . . .


She knew she was living her HAPPILY EVER AFTER because . . .

You know how I love fairy tales! I love to see the transformation – rags to beautiful gowns, pumpkins to coaches! But more so, I love to see how a young girl must overcome her fears and meet some challenges so at the end she lives happily ever after! She does with positive energy, a can-do attitude, and sometimes . . . like for Cinderella . . . the fairy godmother adds a little magic!

Below are stories by some of the women I have worked with. You'll see how the stories – almost inadvertently because there are no coincidences! – follow **The Road Map for the Journey to the Real YOU!™**. That is how natural a human process this manifesting is!

I have included first the writing prompts that the women used in telling their stories so you can write one of your own, too, in your Thriver Zone Journal. This template for "Manifesting – A Fairy Tale" with the writing prompts is also on my website, ThriverZone.com, under the Resources tab.

## ENJOY!

When you are done, we'll move on to the last two chapters of this book – "Creating a Life of Purpose" and "Reclaiming Your Power."

Can't wait to get you on this journey!

## MANIFEST YOUR DESIRES: THRIVER SUCCESS STORIES

Here are some stories about doing something you thought you couldn't do, but you did!

> *ONCE UPON A TIME there was a girl who thought she couldn't get out of the job she had because she didn't have the "right" degrees or credentials.*
>
> *She tried to be positive and searched high and low online to find the right opportunity. And she tried to reach out to friends and others she knew who worked in the same field. And she tried again, but nothing seemed to open the door to the opportunity she sought.*
>
> *There were negative voices in her head telling her that she didn't have what it took. She couldn't earn more money than what she was making.*
>
> *She decided not to listen to such negativity and instead believed that an opportunity was out there waiting for her. She was smart, talented, and had a lot to offer others.*

*Instead she listened to other positive voices that told her* she was good at what she did and those she had helped in her current job that had thanked her for making a difference in their lives.

*When she was done, she felt* humble, courageous, and confident.

*She knew she felt her power when she* got an unexpected call to apply for the type of job she wanted. *Her experience taught her* that when she believes in what she wants and is open to the opportunity, it will yield the result she wants.

*Because of this success, she learned more about her purpose in life,* which is to help others listen for their own inner truth and find what holds them back.

*She knew she was living her HAPPILY EVER AFTER because* she now works in a place where she gets to make a difference in the lives of others, and she loves what she does.

*– YVETTE*

---

*Once upon a time there was a woman* who had a dream to heal people by starting her own USDA organic vegetable and fruit farm. *She tried* telling others about her idea, but they thought it would be too much work and she should be doing other things with her life. *She tried* talking to the local extension people, who told her an organic farm would be a good thing, but it would be a lot of work and she'd have to follow a lot of rules and regulations. *And she tried* asking her neighbors, friends, and family for help clearing and planting the field. Then she attended a Thriver workshop that taught her to overcome her fears, and she got tremendous energy.

*There were negative thoughts in her head telling her* it was too much work. How could she do everything that was needed to run a farm? It would mean clearing the land, starting her own seeds, and planting, watering, weeding, harvesting, and selling her produce. How could she do it all alone?

*She decided not to listen to the negative thoughts in her head* and started the farm anyway. She applied for organic certification and got certified right away. She made cold frames and planted her seeds. She tilled the soil with her loader/backhoe and raked out the one-acre garden. Her husband thought she was crazy.

*"This is too much work for you," he said.*

**Instead she listened to other positive voices that told her** to keep working anyway and do whatever was needed to get each job done. The first year there was enough food for family, friends, neighbors, and a roadside stand. She had overcome all the obstacles, the hard work, and the naysayers and produced wholesome, nutritious food for herself and others. She felt happy and like a woman of power, but this was just the beginning.

**She knew she felt her power when she** opened her second and third planting fields. She now brings fresh organic produce to three large farmers' markets, sells shares of her harvest to local families, sells to restaurants, cafeterias, and organic markets, and donates regularly to the local food pantry.

**Her experience taught her** to never give up on your dream. It is going to take a lot of hard work, research, and many to-do lists, but all things are possible. There will always be someone who will support you when you really need help.

**Because of this success, she learned more about her purpose in life,** which is to bring clean, wholesome, nutritious food to her local community and educate the community regarding organic sustainable practices.

**She knew she was living her HAPPILY EVER AFTER** because now she is thinking about planning health events at the farm, is a member of the local Agricultural Commission, attends regular events to teach people about USDA organic produce, has taught her first organic gardening workshop, and has exceeded her sales goals each year. Her naysayers are now her "yay"-sayers, and she is well-regarded by her local farming community.

*– VIRGINIA*

———————————————————————

**ONCE UPON A TIME there was a girl who thought she couldn't** speak in front of a crowd of people. She had such a fear of public speaking that she would shake while giving any oral report. But one day at a conference for her health careers club, she was asked to speak on any healthcare topic she wanted.

**She was scared as could be.** She only had minutes to decide before going up to speak in front of 400 people. When she went up on the stage, she spoke on the *workings of the heart for about five minutes. It was the longest five minutes she ever spent!*

*When she was finally done* and walking off the stage, she heard the sound of hands clapping and saw to her amazement everyone in the audience standing up and applauding her. She found out later that she was speaking to a roomful of doctors and nurses. Boy, was she glad she didn't know that ahead of time! Now she isn't afraid anymore and enjoys speaking, reading, and praying at church.

*I am woman, hear me roar! I can do anything I put my mind to because I know have courage, acceptance, pride, hope, and faith. When I set my mind on something, I can accomplish it.*

*– NANCY*

---

*ONCE UPON A TIME* there was a girl who thought she couldn't earn a college degree.

*There were negative voices in her head telling her* that she had never been a great student in high school and barely scraped by with Cs when she took an English course at the local community college. When she was asked to write a paper for that class, the voices in her head told her that nothing she wrote would make any sense. When asked to do an oral presentation in class, her fear got the best of her and she dropped out of school. A few years later, she considered returning to school. Then the negative voices told her she'd never be able to complete college courses while she was working. The voices reminded her of how she failed in the past, and what made her think she could pass even one course now?

*She decided not to listen to them* and signed up for an English and Psychology class this time.

*Instead she listened to other positive voices* that told her that she was smart and hardworking. She had a fierce determination when she truly wanted something. She believed that she could handle these courses and any others she might want to take in the future.

*She knew she felt her power when she* began getting As and Bs on her tests and papers in both classes. At the end of the semester, not only did she pass the two *classes, but she also made the Dean's List! That semester because the catalyst to work towards her associate's degree.*

***Her experience taught her*** *that not only could she succeed in school, but she could do it all while working and living on her own.*

***And she knew she was living her HAPPILY EVER AFTER*** *of being an independent woman who could accomplish anything she set her mind to.*

*– JODIE*

———————————————————————

***ONCE UPON A TIME there was a girl who thought she couldn't*** *go back to college, succeed in the professional world, or make a difference in people's lives. She longed to help others, to educate and teach people to believe in themselves, but the problem was that she had learned not to believe in herself.*

***She tried*** *to help others in small ways. She homeschooled her children, teaching them that they could do anything and could succeed, even while still thinking she couldn't.*

***And she tried*** *finding value in her role as a wife and mother, but something in her longed to make a bigger impact on more people's lives.*

***There were negative voices in her head telling her*** *that she wasn't good enough, that no one cared what she had to say, that everyone else was better than her, and she really didn't know anything.*

***She decided not to listen to them*** *by following her dreams and letting her mind wander to greater possibilities. Could she go back to college? She had always loved psychology and studying people's behavior. She knew she would love counseling. This desire to help others became a passion of hers, driving her to push past her fear of failure and apply to college. She researched schools with psychology programs online and found the one school that was at the top of the list. But applying to go to school there seemed like too much for her. She was just a nobody who had nothing of value to offer. So she applied to other schools on the list and, with each acceptance letter that came, she felt a little taller and a little freer. Maybe she was worth something after all! Somebody wanted her! Believed in her! She* *picked a college and started her first class. She felt her mind expand with the joy of learning. She hadn't been in an academic environment for twenty years, and it was exhilarating! She found herself putting energy and passion into her papers for school.*

***She started listening to other positive voices that told her,*** *"God loves you. You are a valuable person. You have had tremendous experiences that other people could learn from. You are wise, strong, and smart, and you can do it." When her professor told her that her writing was at a graduate level, she felt like she was soaring! She could do this! The professional arena had accepted her and thought she had value! No more would those crazy memories of people telling her she was worthless be allowed to surface. She was thriving!*

***She knew she felt her power when she*** *decided to apply to the best school for psychology, the top school she didn't think she could get into before. Getting accepted there was a milestone that made her feeling like she was soaring. She could do anything!*

***Her experience taught her*** *to believe in herself, have courage, step out in faith and trust in what God had planned for her all along. She needed to break through the barriers that the negative voices had placed in her path.*

***And because of this success, she learned more about her purpose in life which is*** *to inspire others to find this freedom and power in believing that they can do anything they choose! Her energy now propelled her on to accomplish more and more of her dreams. Master's degree? Doctorate? She could DO IT!*

***And she knew she was living her HAPPILY EVER AFTER because*** *she felt full of joy. Courage had taken the place of fear, and there wasn't anything life could throw at her that she couldn't handle now. Her world was an open-ended realm of possibilities. Dreams flooded her mind about what her future held. She looked forward to the day she would become a counselor and encourage other women to find their courageous voice.*

***She dreamed of*** *writing about her experiences to encourage others, and now she could. She saw oppression everywhere she looked – in the church, in society, in the court system – and she wanted to do something about it.*

*She vowed to bring justice and hope* to the lives of other victims of abuse, creating in them the desire for thriving, not just surviving what had happened to them. She knew she had lost the feeling of thriving for a while because of what happened to her. But she found it now and would never let go of it again!

*– CATHRYN*

***

*ONCE UPON A TIME there was a girl who thought she couldn't* do anything. She wanted to because an aromatherapist, but she didn't think she was smart enough to do the work. She thought she was too stupid and would never be able to understand it. Everyone said she would never get it.

*She tried and tried and tried again, but there were negative voices in her head telling her that* she was a failure and wouldn't be able to do it. The schools were too far away, she didn't have transportation, and she couldn't move. The courses would take too long to finish, and she wouldn't have the finances to do it. She decided not to listen to her fears, and instead put one foot in front of the other and found out about online schools that she could attend. She also researched how much time it would take for her to complete the training and whether she could use her veterans benefits.

*She kept telling me herself* that she was good enough and she could do well in school because it was a passion of hers that would make her feel joyful and happy. She believed that one day she would open her own business and enjoy working in on aromatherapy, nutrition, reiki, and therapeutic touch. She felt confident and strong in her skills and abilities. She believed that her business would be very busy and productive.

*Then she felt powerful* – happy, brave, strong, and motivated. One day, she would have her own business and live her *HAPPILY EVER AFTER!*

*– JEAN*

***

*ONCE UPON A TIME there was a girl who thought she couldn't* ever be married again. She was divorced twice and was meeting a lot of ugly frogs with ugly attitudes and behaviors.

*She tried* to meet and spend time with men who approached her; she never chose them. *Then she tried* a different approach. She took out newspaper ads, but they didn't work out. *She tried again* by going to single dances and online dating where she assertively had to tell one guy not to turn everything she wrote into a sexual innuendo. He disappeared fast.

*There were negative voices in her head* telling her that she wasn't an interesting person. She was unattractive, not glamorous enough, and she'd never marry again. That voice told her she would never have someone who would love, respect, and care about her. *Instead she listened to other positive voices* that she told her she was lovable, kind, smart, and important. And she realized that she was looking for someone who was also kind, smart, and important to her.

*She felt her power* when she asked a man she was dating, "Where do we go from here?" He took her hand gently as they walked along, and she knew that was a start. *She learned* to know what was in her heart and, most importantly, to value herself and share her happiness with someone she loved.

*She knew she was living her happily ever after* when she and her man began to make plans to get married. It just doesn't get any better than that ... or will it? She will be smiling, laughing, and hugging her friends and family at the wedding.

– ROBIN

---

*ONCE UPON A TIME there was a girl who thought she couldn't* leave a relationship that was filled with darkness and her silence. She was numb, but she could still feel the pain. She could see the hurt, yet she was blind. She stayed and tried to hide. At the same time she tried and tried to escape. She kept going back until she was finally fed up. She gave it all her strength and courage. She was no longer mute.

*There were negative voices in her head telling her* she would be a bad mother if she left and a huge fool if she stayed. *She decided not to listen to them* by taking care of herself, embracing and loving herself, indulging and believing in herself.

*Instead she listened to the positive voice that told her* she didn't do anything wrong and that she could leave. She could do this. She was an intelligent and strong.

*When she finally left and the relationship was done, she felt powerful and hopeful.* She had faith and no longer felt like a prisoner. She had ambition to do all the things the dark had been holding her back from. She was able to walk freely with her head held high. Her experience taught her never to put herself second, take a stand, and have faith that what she believed was right.

Because of this success, **she learned her purpose in life was** always to do what's right, trust in herself and spread the knowledge that living well is the best revenge!

– *ELIZABETH*

---

*ONCE UPON A TIME there was a girl who thought she couldn't* be loved by a boy. As time went on, when an occasional boy came along, she tried treating him like a king and tried not to say or do anything that would make him disapprove of her. She tried to keep her own needs and thoughts, likes, and dislikes small, be quiet, and stay invisible.

*There were negative voices in her head telling her that* she was weird, strange, fat, boy-crazy, oversensitive, and unattractive.

*She decided not to listen to them by* keeping away from people, reading a lot, eating a lot, daydreaming over songs, and creating her own scenarios in her head that brought forth good feelings within her.

*Over time she listened to other positive voices* that told her she was compassionate, caring, creative, and bright.

*When she was done* (which she feels like she never really is), she felt a sense of toxicity within her fall away, and she longed to be healed. She determinedly began her journey toward acceptance of herself.

*Years passed and one day she knew she felt her power* when she said to her partner: "You may not like this, but I do." And she began to honor her thoughts, *emotions, and spirituality by moving closer to taking ownership of herself. **Her** **experience taught her** that rebirth is possible even if your spirit has been shattered, and the lessons learned often come in the guise of self-care.*

***Because of this success, she learned more about her purpose in life,** which is to tell the wounded and damaged ones that IF THEY'VE LOVED, THEY'VE SUCCEEDED.*

***And she knew she was living her happily ever after** because she wrote and read out loud this story to a group of women that she considered her soul sisters.*

*– LYNNE*

---

***ONCE UPON A TIME there was a girl who thought she couldn't** live independently.*

***She tried** to do things on her own without her parents.*

***And she tried** to be optimistic that everything would work out and that she would get to be independent.*

***And she tried again** to trust the steps needed to get to her goal.*

***But there were negative voices in her head telling her,** "You will never move out. You will never have a job. You'll be stuck forever."*

***She decided not to listen to them by** telling herself when she was ready, it would happen. She had to trust Mom and the process. She would soon be able to do the things she wanted to do.*

***Instead she listened to other positive voices that told her** "You are smart, brave, beautiful. Look at what you have overcome. You can do anything."*

***When she was done, she felt** powerful, brave and confident.*

***She knew she felt her power when** she reminded herself of all she can do now and what she had overcome in the past.*

*Her experience taught her to* take things day by day, trust in your journey, and don't be hard on yourself.

*And because of this success, she learned more about her purpose in life which is* to put a smile on the faces of the kids at work.

*And she knew she was living her HAPPILY EVER AFTER because* she lives on her own now with a fun job. She can get out of bed every morning and quiet the negative voice in her head.  Now she can do anything!

*– MALLORY*

––––––––––––––––––––––––––––––

*ONCE UPON A TIME there was a girl who thought she couldn't* return to and maintain a healthy weight.  From childhood to the end of high school, she wore "slim fit" clothes. She was never fat. But later in life, maintaining a healthy weight was difficult for her.

*She tried* from one year to the next at her annual physicals to move the needle on the scale to a lower weight. **And she tried** to go to the gym, increase her physical activity, and make changes in the food she ate. She didn't want to join programs where she'd have to purchases pre-packaged foods which often have a high sodium content that she wanted to avoid. **And she tried again** to cut carbohydrates and return to a low-carb diet which had successfully helped her take off 30 pounds about 18 years before. But each year, her weight was about the same when she checked in with her doctor.

*There were negative voices in her head telling her,* "You'll never be able to shop at the normal clothing stores again. You'll have to live with being a PLUS size.  You don't have the time or money to go to the gym or any other class. Weight loss programs are so expensive and you won't be able to afford the food to succeed. You won't enjoy the foods."

*She decided not to listen to them by* telling herself that she really was a slender, tall person inside. She longed for the days of childhood when people called her "string bean" or "bean pole." In high school, she was referred to as "statuesque."

**Instead she listened to other positive voices that told her,** *"You've done it before, you can do it again. You must plan and prepare yourself for the second half of your life and stay alive. The time is now. Hey! Your job is offering an employee benefit to join a weight loss program and it's free to start. So why not try?" With all that positive energy, she joined the program in January and her goal that year was to lose 50 pounds.*

**When she was done, she felt** *so successful that she told herself she was never going back to her higher weight. Confidently she set next year's goal and she used all the tools she had learned about weight loss to achieve her goal and to help others on their journey. She was grateful to God for answering her prayers.*

**She knew she felt her power when she** *was sought out by others who told her: "You are my inspiration!" "Tell me everything you ate today!" "How does the program work?" "We want to try it too!"*

**Her experience taught her** *to try and try again. Accept small setbacks and get right back on track. Keep negative thoughts and self-talk out. Change what you think about, how you feel and what you do. Shift your perspective. Talk to yourself as you would a friend who you are supportive of and what to see succeed.*

**And because of this success, she has learned** *more about herself. "Don't be so hard on yourself. Make time for yourself. Celebrate both scale and non-scale victories. Work on a new goal for each year and continue to aspire to be a member for life. Celebrate accomplishing your ultimate weight loss goals."*

**She knew she was living her HAPPILY EVER AFTER because** *with her weight loss, every day people would tell her, how nice she looked, how pretty her outfit was, or how much younger she was looking. People would seek her counsel and advice before embarking on their weight loss journey. She felt she could enjoy the second half of her life by maintaining a healthy weight and staying active. Now her stretch goal is to reach her 103rd birthday.*

*– DARLENE*

✑ **PROMPT:** On the same page in your Thriver Zone Journal where you recorded **Map Point A, B, C, D,** write of the desires you have already manifested.

Make a list of the desires you want to manifest next.

What is one obstacle you'll have to overcome to manifest these desires?

Write your plan to take on this obstacle and live your dreams.

~ ~ ~ ~ ~ ~ ~ ~ ~ ~ ~ ~ ~ ~ ~

*We have to reach for things that are beyond our grasp*
*or what is heaven for.*

— GARTH STEIN

*The biggest adventure you can take is to live*
*the life of your dreams.*

— OPRAH WINFREY

*The purpose of life is*

*a life of purpose.*

– Robert Bryne

# Create a Life of Purpose

## WITH CLEAR INTENTION, YOU CAN CREATE THE LIFE YOU WANT!

*Life isn't about finding yourself.*
*Life is about creating yourself.*
— GEORGE BERNARD SHAW

**W**hat I have learned in my life is that a desire for a lot of money or material things can turn into an empty wish that doesn't lead to happiness.

What your desires should take you to are the things you love and the Real YOU loves. So, does that makes it the choice between LOVE or MONEY? Maybe, maybe not, but it is up to you. Of course, you could desire abundance and enough of it so that you'd have the time and money to do many wonderful things that serve humanity!

Look at what people like Oprah Winfrey and Bill and Melinda Gates, who have made billions of dollars, are doing with their money. They are investing it to solve serious problems in the world – including preventing polio in third world countries, opening schools for girls in South Africa – so that they can feed and grow their Real YOU. They have gone beyond merely measuring their success in life financially to living successful lives of purpose.

The best way to see the limitless possibilities that exist for you in the world is to visualize your future in a BIG WAY! You can do it! Do you see a book about your life story on the best-seller list? Have you always wanted to swim with dolphins? Or do you just want you and your kids to have a happy, peaceful life?

Any and all of these dreams can come true! Being abused can make you feel hopeless and derail your dreams. But what you dream about can be yours, particularly if you focus on desires match your values and represent your strongest passions. The Real YOU is your reward in this process. If your focused desire matches your Real YOU –your true values– then when you manifest that desire, you will feel good. The Real YOU can make you feel warm and fuzzy! Once you manifest a dream that matches its value, the positive energy of the Real YOU can fuel your positive energy for the next focused desire you have.

For example, when I started doing workshops to help women who had been abused, I had positive energy and a focused desire to do so. As the workshops became more and more successful, each time I conducted one it fed my Real YOU – doing meaningful work and helping and healing others. Soon I had a new, even more focused desire. This time I wanted to write a book about the work I was doing and spread the Thriver message to more and more women. Yes, I had a lot of fear about whether I could do it, but I used positive energy and unlimited beliefs about myself, such as "I can do this!" to guide me through and break down that wall of fear and resistance.

With each of those desires that I manifested – first to conduct a workshop, then to write a book, followed by other books, and now doing speaking and training about the work that I do – I am building a life of purpose that feeds my Real YOU. I am doing the work I love, and I am helping and healing others. I am doing it with integrity and expanding my knowledge and scope with each new desire I manifest.

It won't surprise you, if you did THE EXERCISE: Choosing What's Important to You in the Finding the Real YOU chapter of this book, that here's what I discovered:

My top three #1s (Most Important – Must Have) are:

**Helping and Healing Others**
**Doing Meaningful Work**
**Having Integrity**

Among my top #2 (Less Important – Nice to Have) on the list are:

**Accomplishing Something**
**Learning New Things**
**Adding New Skills**
**Doing Good Work**
**Excellence**

My #3s (Least Important – Don't Need) are:

**Having a Lot of Status and Prestige**
**Having Power**

No surprises here! My desires are matching up with my Real YOU! I'm on my way to a life of purpose!

So how do you get to a life of purpose? I'd suggest start by manifesting your desires. You now know how to do that with ***The Road Map to the Real YOU!™*** described in this book. In that process, you may see not only where those desires lead you, but also how manifesting one desire gives you more positive energy and focus to take on the next desire. Keep matching your desires to your Real YOU. You want to keep feeding the Real YOU with the things you love.

While I have been working on finding my life of purpose, I've also been watching the women I've worked with begin to carve out lives of purpose. Adrienne, for example, who we met earlier in this book, comes to mind. She has been on her journey to thriving ever since I met her five years ago. She has been writing her story and earning a degree in energy therapy, and she has a new business. She has gained positive energy in her life, focused her desires, pushed through her fears, and found the work that exhilarates her Real YOU! True manifesting!

Manifesting her desires one by one, Adrienne is building a life of purpose with her business that combines Laughter Yoga, Integrated Energy Therapy™, Reiki, and Essential Oils. Laughter Yoga, an exercise routine combining unconditional laughter with Yogic breathing (pranayama), is where Adrienne started. She writes:

Laughter Yoga was the first energy healing therapy that raised my energy and helped me heal from low self-esteem and the abuse I experienced in my life. It reminded me that I am a Thriver! When I am laughing I cannot feel sad, depressed, or angry. Laughter Yoga led me to Integrated Energy Therapy™, Reiki, Angel Card Reading, and Medicinal Aromatherapy. Now I am pursuing a career in Energy Therapy and Aromatherapy.

In January of each year, the women in my Thriver community create a vision board with words and images that express their goals for the coming year. Here's how Adrienne manifested some of her vision board goals to demonstrate Laughter Yoga at a fund-raising event. She explained:

> *I fulfilled every one of the words I put on my vision board at the fund-raising event. I relied on my strength and got the courage to go to this event, ignoring my Inner Critic. I was brave, speaking, "actin' a fool," and getting a room full of women to laugh with me to raise their energy. This is the key to thriving no matter what our circumstances are. I shared parts of my soul that have been missing for a long time. These pieces of soul are so happy to be reunited with the rest of me that they want to come out and play and share the joy of being whole and complete.*

## THE EXERCISE: A $10 MILLION ANSWER

Here's an exercise that can help you get a clearer idea what your life of purpose might be. Do you ever wonder what you would do if you had no constraints and a lot of money? We did this exercise earlier in the book under "What Would I Do If . . ." Let's look at what you wrote then and see if you can go deeper now into what you are passionate about. Write again from this prompt in your Thriver Zone Journal and see what you can find out about what really makes your heart sing! This is an opportunity for your Happy Person Inside to have her say!

✒ **PROMPT:** If I had $10 million and all the time to do whatever I wanted, I'd . . .

Let's review some of the desires you put on your list in answer to this prompt. Does it look something like this list?

**SAMPLE LIST:**

Travel with my family

Buy a house

Pay off my bills

Go back to school

Start a business

Open a center for women and children

Over the years, I have asked hundreds of women I have worked with to make a list and the results have been amazingly like the sample above. Yet, even as they make this list, most of these women don't believe that any of these desires would ever be possible in their lives. Some will tell me that it's impossible because they are too old or too young, don't have the money to achieve them, or simply have no idea how to manifest their desires. It seems beyond their reach, and they have no hope of things changing in the short- or long-term.

Why is it that, though we can imagine wanting these things in our life and even write them down, we still have no real belief they can happen? They are indeed focused desires, they are specific, and for some people they are very doable. Why not for all of us? What keeps us from living our dreams?

## THE EXERCISE: VISION A NEW LIFE

One thing I believe will help us live the life of our dreams is to create a vision incorporating all our positive thoughts and dreams for that future.

✒**PROMPT:** Write about a point in the future as if you are living it now in the present. Describe it in this way: "I'm sitting on the deck of my new vacation home overlooking the ocean on a perfect, sunny day . . ."

Since you are going to do this in the Happy Person frame of mind, this is your BEST-CASE SCENARIO for the future! Make it big and positive! Close your eyes for a minute, if you feel comfortable doing that, and imagine that you are moving from this space in time to the future.

Go forward into next week . . .

next month, next year . . .

three, four, five, or more years ahead . . .

See yourself sometime in your future when all your dreams have come true! You are happy, healthy, and feeling good! LIFE IS REALLY, REALLY GOOD!

Let yourself be there for a moment, noticing where you are, who is with you, and how it all feels. When you are ready, open your eyes, and write in your journal or notebook.

Here's a great vision from one of the women I have worked with. This piece flowed after she wrote the Happy Person Inside Letter in the previous chapter **Map Point A** – Getting Positive Energy.

Remember Tawanda, who wanted to be a doctor one day? Here is what she envisions for the future. Wow!

*Wow, so much is going on right now! The kids are ready. I can hear all the footsteps. Oh! Look at the lights on the chandelier. They are glistening!*

*It smells so beautiful! I did it. I'm at a banquet hall with my children, sisters, and best friend. They are finishing up with the last-minute setup (balloons, microphones, flower assortment). My face is so clear and brown. (My new business photos came out really nice.) I'm celebrating the opening of my strip mall. I have an office space for my private practice, and there is also a daycare center, a hair salon, and a diner with a playscape.*

*I am so psyched. I have lost a lot of weight, and I look good; I'm rocking these nice heels. I am the owner of my own businesses that I've dreamt of for some time. My sisters are all together, happy and ready to get started. I'm so overjoyed to have our home customized just how I want it. It has a huge yard that my sons keep up.*

*We are celebrating our family's success together without the additives (alcohol, cigarettes, and marijuana). It's so great to finally be comfortable and relax.*

*The show is amazing! My son is singing to me while my two other kids are dancing. I'm in tears because they have accomplished their goals within the music industry. I light up when they announced my name as a "doctor." As we cut the ribbon for the grand opening of the strip mall, my kids looked over and said, "See, Mommy, now you're rich. You did it!" I reply, "We have always been rich; now we are comfortable." I owe my thanks to all the people who took time out of their lives to help me figure out mine. I appreciate and love you all.*

## FIND YOUR PURPOSE IN THE REAL YOU

Here's what I have learned from these exercises and the work I have done finding my own life of purpose:

- The most successful people are not the most talented or the smartest.
- They are the ones who are most motivated to overcome their fears and take on huge risks to achieve their success.
- They embrace their lives and the work they do because it is their life of purpose. They are following their passions and living their dreams.
- They do not live in a world of limiting beliefs about themselves, their talents, their value, or their worth.

We can do and feel that way too. We are thrivers! We can make desires come true, connect with the Real YOU inside us, and find our purpose in this lifetime.

Our limitless beliefs about ourselves include:

- **I can create a new life for myself and avenge the abuse I have experienced.**
- **I can find meaningful work that I love and a creative, active life that I long for.**
- **I can live a life of purpose and power NOW!**

Here are some more affirmations the women I've worked with have shared with me over the years. Find the ones that resonant the most for you. Which have the most energy? Recite them every day. Take black marker and write them on sticky notes, and then put them around your house.

Live with them! Breathe them! Let them inhabit your every thought! Make them part of your life! They can help you manifest your desires and get you on track to discover a life of purpose. You can do this!

| | |
|---|---|
| I have my priorities. | I am courageous. |
| I am amazing! | I am smart and strategic. |
| I can do this! | I am competent. |
| I am healthy. | I am blessed. |
| I am a good mother | I put me first! |
| I make healthy food choices. | I am taking care of business. |
| I am doing it! | I am free! |
| I am successful! | I have power, passion, and desire. |
| I run with my passions! | I can create the life I want to live! |
| I broke the silence about abuse in my life. | I am courageous! |
| I am a seeker. | I am on a journey to discovery! |
| I love my journey! | I love the choices I have made. |
| No more crap! | I tell it like it is! I speak my truth. |
| I go with the flow! | Let me be! I love me! |
| Give me space! | I am a good mother! I am great! |
| I'm too much! | I deserve the best! |
| I am fearless of failure! | I am a problem solver! |
| I'm breaking the cycle of abuse in my life. | I am prosperous! |
| I'm strong! I'm invincible! I am woman! | |

You are a thriver! Every day you can fuel your life with positive energy, focus your desires, push through your fears, and find the Real YOU!

You can manifest your dreams and live a life of purpose!

✎ **PROMPT:** On the same page in your Thriver Zone Journal where you recorded **Map Point A, B, C, D** and **the desires you have manifested –**

Make a list of your passions and interests that can lead to your life of purpose.

What motivates you to pursue those passions and interests?

How far along are you in finding a life of purpose?

Write your plan to find your life of purpose and live your dreams.

~ ~ ~ ~ ~ ~ ~ ~ ~ ~ ~ ~ ~ ~

*The purpose of life is to live it, to taste experience to the utmost, to reach out eagerly for newer and richer experience.*

— ELEANOR ROOSEVELT

The very nature of the mind is

such that if you only leave it

in its unaltered and natural state,

it will find its true nature,

which is bliss and clarity.

— SOGYAL RINPOCHE
*THE TIBETAN BOOK OF LIVING AND DYING*

# Reclaim Your Power After Abuse and Loss

*The most common way people give up their power is*
*by thinking they don't have any.*
— ALICE WALKER

I am a Woman of Power

*There are two powers in the world; one is the sword and the other is the pen.*
*There is a third power stronger than both, that of women.*
— MALALA YOUSAFZAI

Can women can permanently break the cycle of abuse and violence in their lives? Can they empower themselves and take charge of their lives? Why is empowerment so important to women who have experienced the power and control of an abusive, violent relationship?

Dr. Judith Herman suggests in her groundbreaking 1992 book, *Trauma and Recovery,* that empowerment is a critical piece for victims of trauma. She states that the core experiences of trauma are disempowerment and disconnection with others. Therefore, recovery is based on the empowerment of the survivor and the creation of new connections. (See more about Dr. Herman's book in the Resources section of this book.)

I view this process to mean that for women who suffer significant emotional trauma or "life-altering events" such as violence and abuse, there is either a road to recovery – a reconnection that brings new vigor and purpose to their lives – or a spiraling down into a debilitating cycle of anger, depression, and hopelessness.

The work I have done for many years with hundreds of women who have experienced abuse – whether it was domestic violence, sexual assault, child abuse, or any other abuse – has shown me that it is only by reconnecting with themselves, their dreams, and a future free of abuse and violence that these women will heal and become truly alive again.

Reclaiming their lives after abuse is the power and destiny of these women, and I have been a witness to their transformations. What a gift!

## THE POWER OF ONE, THE POWER OF ALL

What I learned early on in working with women who have come through abuse is that so much more than abuse and violence has happened to them. All of them have lost, at least temporarily, the dream of having a loving, tender intimate relationship with a partner or spouse, and that's horrific enough. But they have also lost so much more – self-confidence, self-esteem, and the opportunity to grow and prosper.

Those of us who have experienced the effects of abuse have so much to worry about – our children, keeping our families together, getting or keeping a job, and so on. The abusers have tried to take so much away from us – in my case even my beloved niece – but we come back ever stronger. We are living well, seeking our best revenge, and finding the Real YOU inside us. We are forever free and vigilant. This won't happen to us again, we pledge, and we have found a community that feeds and nourishes us so that it won't. And we will bring more and more women along with us so we can fulfill our dream that no one will ever be lost and alone again, unable to find a refuge where there is no judgment about what has come before. Instead we will know the goodness of what will come tomorrow – the sweetness of finding out who we really are and seeing all the lost opportunities as gifts that will propel us quickly and safely to that place of bliss, true happiness, and pure joy!

I am in the glorious company of women who have known abuse and pain but have not only survived but are thriving in the new life they are carving out for themselves, their children, and their families.

I have watched these women transform into amazing women doing amazing things. They are not the same people they were when I first met them. They have given me the gift of being able to watch them transform – sometimes literally right before my eyes – from victim to survivor to thriver! This work has assured me that my niece Maggie not only will be remembered, but also that her legacy will live on in the lives of all the women I have been privileged to work with and touch with a message of thriving!

When you have completed this book, I hope you will feel much more empowered and confident in your ability to move forward and complete your journey to the Real YOU.

Let's write a "Woman of Power" statement for you.

## THE EXERCISE: CRAFT A WOMAN OF POWER STATEMENT

What's most important about this statement is that what you write is short, to the point, and without any "limiting" words. It's not what we are "trying to" or "will" do to find our power. We are powerful right now! Stick with strong, active words in the present tense.

✎ **PROMPT:** Make a list of your POWER words.

> *FOR EXAMPLE:*
> **Limitless, Free, Fearless, Active, Passionate, Audacious, Courageous, Brave, Honest, Daring, Dynamic, Bold, Energized, Inspired, Motivated, Persistent, Dogged, Perseverance, Strong, Mighty, No-Nonsense**

Now go back and take a look at the list you created in **EXERCISE: Choosing What's Important to You** in Finding the Real YOU section of this book. Go through that list of words that describe in positive, glowing terms the Real YOU – the Thriver in you.

Think about all these items and use them to craft your "I am a Woman of Power." Mine is below as a sample. Once you have yours done, read it every day! Post it somewhere where you'll see it often. I keep mine near my computer monitor so I won't forget it.

✒ **PROMPT:**  I am a woman of power who . . .

Today I celebrate my life by . . .

I have given this assignment to many women in my Thriver community over the years, and what the women have written has always been amazing! First, here's mine.

> **I am a woman of power whose mission in life is to be a catalyst for change for victims of violence against women. Today I celebrate my life by building a community of strong, independent, productive women who have survived abuse and are thriving in well-being, love, and joy.**

One of my favorite "I Am a Woman of Power" statements from the women I've worked with was created by Sophia, a woman who attended one of my first workshops. At many of our Thriver events, Sophia is regularly asked to read her "I Am a Woman of Power" statement. We not only love it, we love how she reads it with power and grace! Here it is:

> *I am a woman of power who has made a positive impact on the world through my own healing, wellness, and creativity.*
>
> *I am a woman of power who has integrity and always believes in doing the right thing, even when it is challenging. It exposes my true character when no one sees me but God.*
>
> *I am a woman of power who has embarked upon this earth to make a difference in other women's lives, to inspire them to achieve their highest level of humanity, and cultivate the world with love.*
>
> *Today I celebrate my life by being true to myself, being open to others, and being filled with positive energy. This transformation has brought out the best in me, taught me self-love, and, like a flower bud, allowed me to blossom into a beautiful rose.*
>
> *Today I celebrate my life, which resembles the ever-changing four seasons – fall to winter, winter to spring, and then spring to summer – secure that I can go forward with confidence and without fear of anything.*
>
> *– SOPHIA*

This Woman of Power statement is so fabulous because it not only shows how Sophia is no longer silent, but it also shows the power of women like Sophia who are transforming their lives and finding their true purpose. Let's celebrate the Woman of Power statements below by a number of women who have also worked with me and are now part the Thriver community.

## I AM A WOMAN OF POWER STATEMENTS

*I am a woman of power who can heal myself and love myself unconditionally.*

*I am a woman of power who can show my children that I can have a happy and peaceful life at any age.*

*I am a woman of power who has confidence in myself. I am my own best friend.*

*– ADRIENNE*

~ ~ ~ ~ ~ ~ ~ ~ ~ ~ ~ ~ ~ ~ ~ ~ ~ ~ ~ ~ ~

*I am a woman of power who no longer is silent, who no longer is crushed. I will speak up. The most important lesson is that I must do it myself; I am no longer afraid.*

*I am a woman of power, and the gifts I possess and the values that have shaped me will control my future now.*

*I am a woman of power, and I trust that when I look up to the skies, someone is watching over me.*

*– SUSAN P.*

~ ~ ~ ~ ~ ~ ~ ~ ~ ~ ~ ~ ~ ~ ~ ~ ~ ~ ~ ~ ~

*I am no longer a child victim to her father's touch,*

*Or a girlfriend obeying and performing just to hold on*

*I am no longer*

*A wife fulfilling my marital duties*

*Or a mother obsessed with providing for her children trying to make up for failing at her marriage.*

*I am a woman*

*I am a woman with power*

*I am a woman of power!*

*I leave my own footprints in the sand,*

*Deciding each day what path is right for me.*

*I am a woman of power*

*Articulating my own thoughts,*

*Not just the ones I think you want to hear.*

*I am a woman of power*

*Understanding that our opinion and feelings may differ*

*And I am okay with that*

*In fact, I embrace our differences.*

*I am a woman of power*

*Loving myself,*

*My body*

*My skin*

*And each organ that it holds inside that works tirelessly to give me life.*

*I am a woman of power*

*In charge of your touch,*

*Open to your embrace*

*And learning every day*

*The beauty of safe, loving touch.*

*I stand before you*

*Strong and tall*

*Loud and proud as I proclaim*

*I am woman of power*

*With a newfound passion*

*Seeking to help other women*

*Discover their internal power.*

*Because, my friend, we all have the right and the ability*

*To be a woman with power,*

*To be a woman of power.*

*– TERI*

~ ~ ~ ~ ~ ~ ~ ~ ~ ~ ~ ~ ~ ~ ~ ~ ~ ~ ~ ~ ~ ~

*I am a woman of power who now enjoys the simple joys of life and who would like to share my love of life with those who have less opportunity. I can say no to drama!*

*I am a woman of power who would enjoy teaching self-love to both boys and girls.*

*Today I celebrate my life by enjoying each moment and letting go of things that do not matter and cannot be changed.*

*– THERESE*

~ ~ ~ ~ ~ ~ ~ ~ ~ ~ ~ ~ ~ ~ ~ ~ ~ ~ ~ ~ ~ ~

*I am a woman of power who is moving forward and learning to take care of myself, guiding my children and showing them what the values of life should be.*

*Today I am learning how to carry myself with self-respect, and I am helping others with what I have learned from my past experiences. I am showing them the benefits of having a peaceful life within your heart and how then everything just seems to fall into place. In accepting our failures, we give ourselves the energy to move forward to a successful life.*

*Today I celebrate that my life belongs to me. No longer living in the fear of darkness, rising above the ashes with the warmth of the light guiding me. Having peace, joy, and happiness fulfilling and completing my heart.*

*– DONNA*

*P.S. It's been six years since I wrote this piece, and I can guarantee you that your life will get better. In fact, my life has never been so wonderful. For any woman reading this book, you may doubt that you can change your life or that you can do this. Let me be living proof that not only can you do this, but also that your life will change and can be wonderful. It can be whatever you want it to be. You are the commander of your life, and by leaving an abusive relationship, you can take your life back and live it as it was meant to be. No one else has the right to be your commander except you. I'm not saying it will always be easy, but with great challenges come great rewards. Seek and reach out to people, including your family and friends, and most importantly, to organizations for domestic violence victims so they can support and guide you. You can have your life back and be reborn into the life you were meant to live. If I can do it, anyone can!*

*– DONNA*

~ ~ ~ ~ ~ ~ ~ ~ ~ ~ ~ ~ ~ ~ ~ ~ ~ ~ ~ ~ ~ ~

*To my abuser and every abuser out there: past, present, and future,*

*I am a woman of power, a woman who has been empowered, and I have something to say to you. You thought you could tear me down piece by piece, isolate me, and break my spirit. You thought you could silence my voice and plant the seeds of self-doubt. But the tree that bends and weathers heavy storms grows deeper roots, and bones that break mend stronger.*

*And so too does a woman beaten down and oppressed grow strength and resolve beyond your comprehension, a spirit beyond your grasp, a voice that cannot be silenced, and a zest for life you cannot touch. She is beyond your control, beyond your reproach; and she does it through the unity, strength, and tenacity of all the woman who have suffered in silence with her.*

*We are neither suffering nor silent any longer.*

*We have a voice, and it is clear and strong.*

*We have a goal and the unwavering resolve to achieve it.*

*We will be heard.*

*We will make changes.*

*We will heal the damage you have caused.*

*We will replace your words of hate with love, your lies with truth, and your ridicule with affirmations.*

*We will do this with grace and poise as a coalition of sisters allied in a common front.*

*We are here to tell you that we have had enough.*

*We will put an end to your reign of terror, one woman at a time.*

*We will speak out.*

*We will make people listen.*

*We will make a difference.*

*– JENNY*

~ ~ ~ ~ ~ ~ ~ ~ ~ ~ ~ ~ ~ ~ ~ ~ ~ ~ ~ ~ ~ ~

## LIVING YOUR LIFE AS A WOMAN OF POWER!

Aren't these "I Am a Woman of Power" Statements amazing? Can't you feel the energy coming off the page? Let's think about ways you can own your power and use it to propel your life forward as an empowered woman!

✎ **PROMPT:** On the same page in your Thriver Zone Journal where you recorded **Map Point A, B, C, D** and where you listed your **manifested desires** and goals of your **life of purpose,** write down first your power words and then your "I Am a Woman of Power" Statement.

Your statement should grow and change over time. Maybe you'll add to it to make it more powerful. Or you could shorten it so that it really packs a wallop!

In any case, write now from these prompts:

- How will I hold on to my power every day?

- What will I do when I feel myself losing my power?

- How can I embrace my power and move my life forward?

## GO FORWARD INTO A THRIVER LIFE

Finding your power and purpose can lead you forward into the life of a thriver.

Let's read our definition of a thriver one more time.

*A thriver is a happy, self-confident and productive individual who believes she has a prosperous life ahead of her. She is primed to follow her dreams, go back to school, find a new job, start her own business, or write her story. She believes in herself and in her future so much that she will not return to an abusive relationship. She speaks knowledgeably and confidently about her experiences and is not stuck in her anger or need for revenge.*

*Living well is her best revenge!*

Going forward into the land of your dreams means living the life the Real YOU wants for you. It is going forward that also brings on healing, makes healthy relationships possible, and creates a life of pure joy, peace, and freedom.

May you enter the Thriver Zone and stay there to find your perfect life, your Happy Ending. It is waiting for you! Living well is your best revenge and the fulfillment of all your dreams! Enjoy!

~ ~ ~ ~ ~ ~ ~ ~ ~ ~ ~ ~ ~ ~

*Remember forward movement.*
*Forward is the way of trust.*
*Forward is the way of forgiveness.*
*Forward is the way of action.*
*Forward is the way of healing.*
*Forward is essentially healing.*
— VICTORIA ERIKSON

*All that spirits desire, spirits attains.*
— KHALIL GIBRAN

*Just when the*

*caterpillar*

*thought the*

*world was over,*

*it became a*

*butterfly.*

— PROVERB

# The Thriver Survival Kit

*My mission in life is not merely to survive, but to thrive;*
*And to do it with some passion, some compassion,*
*some humor, and some style*
— MAYA ANGELOU

*Living well is the best revenge!*
— GEORGE HERBERT

To close this book, entitled *Staying in the Thriver Zone,* I thought it would be fun to consider activities, exercises, and thoughts that keep us in that Thriver energy.

Working with the women over the years in the Thriver community that we have built, I have found that, once we are in the Thriver Zone, we need stay there. How do we do that? I don't have THE answer to that question, but I can tell you that we have found a few things that seem to work.

Take a look at the exercises below in what I will call here the "Thriver Survival Kit" and see what you think. I'd love to know what works for you!

## THE EXERCISE: MAKE A LIST OF WHAT KEEPS YOU THRIVING

Working with women who have taken the journey from victim to survivor to thriver, I have been amazed by what keeps them thriving, even in the face of so many things that could easily distract or send them back to victimhood.

I ask women regularly, "What keeps you thriving? What do you do to keep that Thriver energy going in your life?" The list below is not exhaustive; you can add your own ideas, too.

What time, place, thing, or activity takes you back to the Thriver Zone and keeps you there if you need it?

✍ **PROMPT: Make a list of activities** that you use or might use to keep yourself in the Thriver energy.

Here's a list I have collected of ways the women I've worked with have created calm in their lives and energized themselves to keep moving forward:

Play music, soothing, playful, invigorating – depending on my mood

Do knitting, crocheting

Put together a jigsaw puzzle

Have a cup of hot tea, cocoa

Read O, The Oprah magazine

Eat biscotti, chocolate chip cookies, or ice cream

Dig in the dirt, garden

Get a massage, foot massage

Do yoga

Get some energy work done, such as reiki

Spend time in solitude, silence

Write in a journal

Burn incense

Put on a meditation tape

Play with pets

Spend time with your partner

Spend time with children, grandchildren

Burn a candle or sage. Pick a scent like lavender, vanilla to calm, energize you

Volunteer to work with teens, families, kids

Have fun, share jokes

Watch movies – funny, romantic, adventure, travel

Cuddle a baby

Go outside and look at the stars at night

Look at rocks, seashells you collected at beach

Do scrapbooking

Get some fresh flowers

Go for a walk

Get rid of household clutter

Listen to the sound of ocean waves

Swim in a pool or in the ocean

Listen to water in a fountain

Revisit a good memory

Look at photographs of good times

Take a day trip

Get out of the house and enjoy nature

Take a hike, go for a bike ride

## THE EXERCISE: WRITE A POEM OR PROSE

A poem doesn't have to rhyme. It doesn't have to be a certain length. It could even be only a few lines. What's important is that it can calm you, inspire you, or help you work out a feeling or block of feelings in your mind.

*I have never started a poem yet whose end I knew.*

*Writing . . . is discovering.*

– ROBERT FROST

What is poetry? Here's what a few poets have written about poetry.

*The role of the writer is not to say what we can all say*

*but what we are unable to say.*

— ANAIS NIN

*A poem . . . begins as a lump in the throat, a sense of wrong,*

*a homesickness, a lovesickness . . .*

*It finds the thought and the thought finds the words.*

— ROBERT FROST

*If I feel physically as if the top of my head were taken off,*

*I know that is poetry.*

— EMILY DICKINSON

What is prose? Any other kind of writing that isn't poetry. It could be a short story, a novel, memory, or a journal entry.

*For me, a page of good prose is where*

*one hears the rain and the noise of battle.*

— JOHN CHEEVER

Or it could be a prose poem. What is that? Almost universally, it is not agreed upon, but generally it is a poem that doesn't rhyme or even have a format of a poem.

*A good prose poem is a statement that seeks sanity*

*whilst its author teeters on the edge of the abyss.*

— RUSSELL EDSON

I am regularly blessed with poetry and prose that the women I work with write to express themselves, express their gratitude to me, or just to let some of their feelings out. This thriving stuff is hard work! Sometimes they need a break, and for some, writing is how they blow off steam or simply relax. Their writing is also very inspiring and transformational.

In any case, I am the recipient of some wonderful pieces that I'd like to share with you below. But first, why don't you try the exercise?

✎ **PROMPT: Write a poem or a piece of prose** that describes your journey, what energizes you on your journey, how you express your gratitude for where you are today on your journey – or whatever else comes out in the writing.

Here are some samples from the women I have worked with to inspire you in writing your own unique piece!

~ ~ ~ ~ ~ ~ ~ ~ ~ ~ ~ ~ ~ ~

## I Did It My Way

by Christine

The sun's on my face.

My shadow still follows.

I held the sickle tightly as I sliced away the tall strands of hay.

Where is the path? Where is the way?

I need not follow. I need not stray.

I can lead them and show them the way.

But we all must take up our own sickles and cut our own path to lead the way.

~ ~ ~ ~ ~ ~ ~ ~ ~ ~ ~ ~ ~ ~

## How I Know I Am a Thriver

by Adrienne

I know I am a thriver because I can look at myself the mirror and see a happy face! My eyes are blue again, and there is happiness there now where before there was only gray and sadness. Yes, that's right my eyes have changed back to their God-given color – blue.

My journey has been long, a dozen years. How did I get here? Someone literally took me by the hand to guide me in my first step. At first, I was just a living, breathing body just getting through each day. Those who know can relate. We spend our days just getting by trying not to make our abusers angry, which is impossible, but we try with all our hearts anyway. We raise our children, keep house, make meals, and work but there is no joy and no emotion other than fear.

I know I am a thriver because I now feel joy when I wake up in the morning! Joy! Joy! Joy! Joy to be alive, joy to work, joy to see my children grow to be adults.

I know I am a thriver because I see color in the world again! The world is a rainbow!

I know I am a thriver because I love my body! It is mine, not someone else's to ravage and throw away when they are done with it. I had accumulated sixty pounds of protection which I no longer need and has slipped away. I feel beautiful!

I know I am a thriver because I am able to help others see their beauty! In the abusive situation I could not even help myself, but now I can help others on their journey, and this brings even more joy!

I know I am a thriver because I can laugh again. Not just any kind of laughter – rich belly laughter that oxygenates my brain and my soul, bringing more joy!

I know I am a thriver because I have a deep connection to God! I am connected to all living beings on earth; the angels told me. I see concrete signs of this connection every day!

I know I am a thriver because I am not afraid to dream again! I am the snake; I have shed the skin of fear of my dreams, and they come to me now and provide me messages of joy!

I know I am a thriver because I am grateful for everything in my life, all of it good and not so good. The challenges have helped me be more grateful for the abundance I have now.

I know I am a thriver because I have learned to forgive. Forgiveness of self is the highest mountain to climb; I am almost at the summit. Even forgiveness of the abuser is necessary to thrive. This is the teaching of God, and it is so.

~ ~ ~ ~ ~ ~ ~ ~ ~ ~ ~ ~ ~ ~

## A Year Ago

by Teri

A year ago, I walked into my first workshop

scared, feeling out of place,

and confused.


A year ago, I walked into my first workshop

hoping I was ready

knowing I did not want to disappoint you.


A year ago, I walked into my first workshop

unsure of the process

a stranger to the Happy Person Inside me

knowing I did not fit in

doubting I would ever qualify as a Thriver


Today I step in my world

not so scared,

knowing this is the perfect place for me

and clearly knowing where I want to be


Today I step in my world

knowing I am ready

less worried about disappointing others and acting on my own behalf

Today I step in my world

trusting the process

getting to know the happy person inside me

feeling like sometimes I fit in

and knowing that I do qualify as a Thriver!


Thank you for every ounce of guidance, encouragement, and nudging.

Thank you for helping me discover the Happy Person Inside me

and introducing me to the concept of being a Thriver.

I am in a far better place today, I am more confident

and I can encourage myself to try new things,

For your part in my growth, I am forever thankful.

~ ~ ~ ~ ~ ~ ~ ~ ~ ~ ~ ~ ~ ~

## Looking for Healing

by Tennille

When I met Susan and attended one of her workshops, I was looking for healing.

The experience was great. I have never been to a workshop like this before. We were all there for the same thing; however, our personal experiences were never discussed. There was an unspoken bond that was created by just being in the same room, having the same pain and victories.

The work I did that day has given me more healing and strength and courage. It has "awakened" in me my fears and goals. Now I can face, embrace, and grace them.

I pray that each woman that is in need will somehow stumble onto these workshops – they are so motivational! I am in therapy, but this workshop is an addition to me being on the road to recovery; it was so beneficial to me.

I love Susan, and I ask God to keep blessing her and letting her fight the good fight for all of us!

~ ~ ~ ~ ~ ~ ~ ~ ~ ~ ~ ~ ~ ~

Rome was not built in a day. Some days, I take other roads to build Rome.

I take leaps forward; other days I slip and slide backward.

But I do not look backward; I only look forward.

The chains no longer hold me. I no longer feel them, nor do I hear them.

It is the dawn of a new day; I hear the birds chirping.

The darkness is gone. Bright days are ahead.

– Susan P.

~ ~ ~ ~ ~ ~ ~ ~ ~ ~ ~ ~ ~ ~

## Thriver (noun)

by Jenny

1) A woman with a known fascination with glitter glue committed to making the world a more beautiful place.

2) One who progresses toward or realizes her goals despite circumstances.

3) A person who flourishes and prospers.

4) Someone who has mastery over her inner critic and celebrates the happy person inside her.

Examples:

Wow, those thrivers sure know how to decoupage.

That thriver is going to change the world.

~ ~ ~ ~ ~ ~ ~ ~ ~ ~ ~ ~ ~ ~

*The journey into the miraculous begins here.*
*Now is the best time to start.*
– DEEPAK CHOPRA

# RESOURCES

## CRISIS INTERVENTION

For immediate crisis intervention services in your local community, contact:

- The National Domestic Violence Hotline 1-800-799-SAFE (7233) **www.thehotline.org**

- National Sexual Assault Hotline at 1-800-656-HOPE (4673) **www.rainn.org**

- National Center for Victims of Crime **www.victimsofcrime.org/help-for-crime-victims**

- Office for Victims of Crime, U.S. Department of Justice. **www.ovc.gov**

## DATING VIOLENCE AND STALKING

- Break the Cycle: Empowering Youth To End Dating Violence **www.breakthecycle.org**

- Love Is Respect – National Teen Dating Abuse Help Line 1-866-331-9474 **www.loveisrespect.org**

- End Stalking in America **www.esia.net** provides information and assistance to potential victims and those currently being harassed, including a list of state laws against stalking.

- The Sanctuary for Victims of Stalking **www.stalkingvictims.com** offers sanctuary and resources on stalking to victims, how to identify stalking and deal with it through an online support group.

- Women's Law.org **www.womenslaw.org** is a project of the National Network to End Domestic Violence, providing legal information and support to victims of domestic violence, stalking and sexual assault.

## DOMESTIC VIOLENCE

- National Network to End Domestic Violence (NNEDV) **www.nnedv.org** offers support to victims of domestic violence who are escaping abusive relationships and empowers survivors to build new lives.

- National Coalition Against Domestic Violence (NCADV) **www.ncadv.org** works closely with battered women's advocates around the country to identify the issues and develop a legislative agenda.

- **www.domesticshelters.org** Free, online, searchable database of domestic violence shelter programs nationally.

- National Resource Center on Domestic Violence (NRCDV) **www.nrcdv.org** is a source of information for those wanting to educate themselves and help others on the many issues related to domestic violence.

## SEXUAL ASSAULT

- RAINN — Rape Abuse & Incest National Network **www.rainn.org** operates the National Sexual Assault Hotline and has programs to prevent sexual assault, help Victims, and ensure they receive justice.

- National Sexual Violence Resource Center **www.nsvrc.org** provides leadership in preventing and responding to sexual violence through creating resources and promoting research.

- The Victim Rights Law Center **www.victimrights.or**g is dedicated solely to serving the legal needs of sexual assault victims. It provides training, technical assistance, and in some cases, free legal assistance in civil cases to sexual assault victims in certain parts of the country.

## CHILD ABUSE

- Childhelp USA National Child Abuse **www.childhelp.org** directly serves abused and neglected children through the National Child Abuse Hotline, 1-800-4-A-CHILD® and other programs.

## POST TRAUMATIC STRESS

See information listed at National Institute of Mental Health website, **www.nimh.nih.gov**.

## BOOKS ON JOURNALING AND CREATIVE WRITING

*One to One: Self-Understanding through Journal Writing and Life's Companion:* Journal Writing as a Spiritual Quest by Christina Baldwin

*The Artist's Way: A Spiritual Path to Higher Creativity* by Julia Cameron

*Journal to the Self: Twenty-Two Paths to Personal Growth* by Kathleen Adams

*Writing Down the Bones* by Natalie Goldberg

*Bird by Bird* by Anne Lamont

## BOOKS ON PERSONAL GROWTH AND SPIRITUAL DEVELOPMENT

*Secrets about Life Every Woman Should Know: Ten Principles for Total Emotional and Spiritual Fulfillment* by Barbara De Angelis

*Anam Cara: A Book of Celtic Wisdom* by John O'Donohue

*The Seven Spiritual Laws of Success: A Practical Guide to the Fulfillment of Your Dreams* by Deepak Chopra. Also, The Path to Love and How to Know God

*Care of the Soul and Soul Mates* by Thomas Moore

*A Return to Love and A Woman's Worth* by Marianne Williamson

*Something More: Excavating Your Authentic Self and Simple Abundance* by Sarah Ban Breathnach

*You Can Heal Your Life* by Louise L. Hay

*Sacred Contracts: Awakening Your Divine Potential* by Caroline Myss

*Faith in the Valley: Lessons for Women Who Are on the Journey to Peace* by Iyanla VanZant

*The Gifts of Imperfection: Let Go of Who You Think You're Supposed to Be and Embrace Who You Are* by Brene Brown. Also, view her TED Talks at www.TED.com

*Wherever You Go, There You Are: Mindfulness Meditation in Everyday Life* by Jon Kabat-Zinn

## BOOKS AND WEBSITES TO EDUCATE AND INSPIRE YOU

*It Could Happen to Anyone: Why Battered Women Stay* by Alyce LaViolette and Ola Barnett
**www.alycelaviolette.com**

*Why Does He Do That? Inside the Minds of Angry and Controlling Men and Daily Wisdom for Why Does He Do That?* by Lundy Bancroft www.lundybancroft.com

*Macho Paradox: Why Some Men Hurt Women and How All Men Can Help* by Jackson Katz
**www.jacksonkatz.com**

*Trauma and Recovery: The Aftermath of Violence from Domestic Abuse to Political Terror* by Judith Herman, MD

*Beyond Trauma: A Healing Journey for Women* by Stephanie S. Covington, PhD
**www.stephaniecovington.com**

*I Closed My Eyes: Revelations of a Battered Woman* by Michele Weldon
**www.micheleweldon.com**

*The Verbally Abusive Relationship and Verbal Abuse Survivors Speak Out; On Relationship and Recovery* by Patricia Evans **www.patriciaevans.com**

*From Ex-Wife to Exceptional Life™: A Woman's Journey through Divorce* by Donna Ferber
**www.donnaferber.com**

Miss America by Day: Lessons Learned from Ultimate Betrayals and Unconditional Love by Marilyn Van Debur **www.missamericabyday.com**

*A Thousand Splendid Suns* by Khaled Husseini, author of *The Kite Runner*

*Coercive Control: How Men Entrap Women in Personal Life* by Evan Stark

*Scared Silent: A Memoir* by Mildred Muhammad **www.mildredmuhammad.com**

*Invisible Chains: Overcoming Coercive Control in Your Intimate Relationship* by Lisa Aronson

# MOVIES TO ACCOMPANY YOU ON YOUR JOURNEY

*Wonder Woman* (2017) A woman raised as an Amazon warrior, leaves home to fight a war and in the end, discovers her full powers and true purpose in life.

*Beauty and the Beast* (2017) – Belle is more empowered in this movie version. She likes to read and learn and doesn't want marry a hyper-masculine man.

*Cinderella* (2015) – A newer version with Lily James of Downton Abbey. Best line, "I forgive you!"

*Wild* (2014) with Reese Wetherspoon – True story of Cheryl Strayed, who undertook a 100-mile solo hike as a way to recover from her mother's untimely death.

*Saving Mr. Banks* (2013) – The woman who created the Mary Poppins stories takes on Walt Disney.

*Philomena* (2013) with Judi Dench – Inspiring journey of unmarried mother to uncover truth about the son she was forced to give up decades earlier.

*Frozen* (2013) – A story of an epic journey to help a sister and put an end to her icy spell.

*Sleeping with the Enemy* (1991) with Julia Roberts – An abused woman gets a life!

*Eat, Pray, Love* (2010) with Julia Roberts – A woman's quest to rediscover and reconnect with her true, inner self.

*Enchanted* (2007) with Amy Adams – The ultimate "real-life" fairy tale with a big production number in Central Park, New York City.

*Enough* (2002) with Jennifer Lopez – An abused woman fights back.

*Shallow Hal* (2001) with Gwyneth Paltrow and Jack Black – Beauty lies within.

*Riding in Cars with Boys* (2001) with Drew Barrymore – Based on a true story of a woman's life.

*Paying It Forward* (2000) with Helen Hunt – No good deed goes unrewarded.

*Billy Elliot* (2000) – A young boy finds his dream in ballet despite his father's disapproval.

*Erin Brockovich* (2000) with Julia Roberts – A woman who doesn't give up and helps others!

*Ever After* (Cinderella) (1998) with Drew Barrymore – The best happy ending.

*How Stella Got Her Groove Back* (1998) – Stella takes inventory of her life.

*Titanic* (1997) – Rose lives on to find the life of her dreams.

*Waiting to Exhale* (1995) with Whitney Houston – Be happy with who you are.

*The Color Purple* (1995) with Oprah Winfrey – Based on Alice Walker's novel.

*Muriel's Wedding* (1995) with Toni Colette – The hapless Muriel finds herself!

*What's Love Got to Do With It* (1993) – The triumph of Tina Turner.

*A League of Their Own* (1992) with Madonna and Rosie O'Donnell – A sports story for women!

*Enchanted April* (1991) – Rent a villa in Italy and see what happens.

*Thelma and Louise* (1991) with Susan Sarandon – Girls rock even as they careen in a car over a cliff.

*Fried Green Tomatoes* (1991) – Based on Fanny Flagg's novel about the Whistle Stop Café.

*Cry for Help: The Tracy Thurman Story* (1989) – A true story about overcoming injustice and achieving social change.

*The Burning Bed* (1984), starring Farrah Fawcett – Still a riveting story.

## MUSIC TO SOOTHE YOU

Michael Hoppe: *The Yearning – Romances for Alto Flute* (with Tim Wheater)

  *The Unforgetting Heart, Solace* and *The Poet – Romance for Cello*

Raphael: *Music to Disappear Into I* and *II*

**Movie Soundtracks:** *Possession* and *Secret Garden*

Enya: including *A Day Without Rain* and *Paint the Sky with Stars*

David Lanz: including *Cristofori's Dream*

Loreena McKennitt: including *The Book of Secrets*

Thanks for reading the second book in Susan M. Omilian's Thriver Zone Series™

# *Staying in the Thriver Zone*
## *A Road Map to Manifest Your Power and Purpose*

*Also Available – Susan's first book*
# **Entering the Thriver Zone**
## *A Seven-Step Guide to Thriving After Abuse*

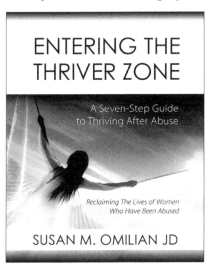

*Coming NEXT in The Thriver Zone Series™!*
# **Living in the Thriver Zone**
## *A Celebration of Living Well as the Best Revenge*

*Connect with Susan about her book and her work with women . . .*
**www.ThriverZone.com**

*Susan's books are available nationally on Amazon.com, BarnesandNoble.com and at your favorite library or local bookstore.*

*Order on Susan's website, www.ThriverZone.com for autographed copies.*

*Contact Susan (susan@thriverzone.com) for bulk purchases at quantity discounts.*

*Now Available*
*Susan's first book in The Best Revenge Series™!*

## Awaken
*The Awakening of the Human Spirit on a Healing Journey*

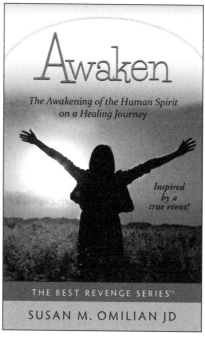

*A story, inspired by true events, that captures
the heart and soul of how women can thrive after abuse.*

*Coming NEXT in The Best Revenge Series™!*
### Emerge and Thrive

*Connect with Susan about her books and her work with women....*
**www.ThriverZone.com**
www.facebook.com/ThriverZone
www.twitter.com/ThriverZone
www.pinterest.com/susanomilian/thriver-zone
www.linkedin.com/in/susanomilian
www.youtube.com/susanom1